Dear Richard,

We hope this book ... and shows you new ways to worship our wonderful God!

Love
Elena, Javi, Natalie, Naomi + Cristian

How Then Shall We Worship?

R.C. SPROUL

How THEN SHALL We WORSHIP?

BIBLICAL PRINCIPLES TO GUIDE US TODAY

HOW THEN SHALL WE WORSHIP?
Published by David C Cook
4050 Lee Vance View
Colorado Springs, CO 80918 U.S.A.

David C Cook Distribution Canada
55 Woodslee Avenue, Paris, Ontario, Canada N3L 3E5

David C Cook U.K., Kingsway Communications
Eastbourne, East Sussex BN23 6NT, England

The graphic circle C logo is a registered trademark of David C Cook.

All rights reserved. Except for brief excerpts for review purposes, no part of this book may be reproduced or used in any form without written permission from the publisher.

The website addresses recommended throughout this book are offered as a resource to you. These websites are not intended in any way to be or imply an endorsement on the part of David C Cook, nor do we vouch for their content.

Unless otherwise noted, all Scripture quotations are taken from the New King James Version®. Copyright © 1982 by Thomas Nelson. Used by permission. All rights reserved. Scripture quotations marked ESV are taken from The Holy Bible, English Standard Version® (ESV®), copyright © 2001 by Crossway, a publishing ministry of Good News Publishers. Used by permission. All rights reserved.

LCCN 2013932963
ISBN 978-1-4347-0424-5
eISBN 978-1-4347-0556-3

© 2013 R. C. Sproul
Published in association with the literary agency of Wolgemuth & Associates, Inc.

First edition published by Reformation Trust Publishing under the title *A Taste of Heaven: Worship in the Light of Eternity* in 2006 © R. C. Sproul, ISBN 978-1-56769-076-7

The Team: Alex Field, Nick Lee, Renada Arens, Karen Athen
Cover Design: Amy Konyndyk
Cover Photo: iStockphoto

Printed in the United States of America
Second Edition 2013

1 2 3 4 5 6 7 8 9 10

022613

For Dr. John MacArthur

CONTENTS

Preface — 9

1 The Form of Worship — 13

2 Sacrifices in Faith — 23

3 Living Sacrifices — 39

4 The House of Prayer — 47

5 Symbolism in Worship — 57

6 Baptism, Part 1 — 65

7 Baptism, Part 2 — 77

8 To You and Your Children — 91

9 The Lord's Supper — 105

10 The Whole Person — 119

11 The Role of Beauty — 131

| 12 | The Sounds of Worship | 141 |
| 13 | The Touch of Eternity | 153 |

Conclusion	165
About the Author	167
Study Guide	169

PREFACE

We observe the flight of birds with a sense of awe. We watch them soar above the trees, wings arching, reaching up to the clouds. Every person has an inbred wish to be able to mimic the birds. Oh, that we could fly unaided, without the assistance of machinery. But it is not our nature to fly. God gifted the birds with inherent abilities and traits to make flying possible. He constructed them with lightweight bones, feathers, and wings that propel them in flight. Still, birds do not fly from the moment they hatch from their eggs. They must mature for a short period in the nest, learning the rudiments of flight from their parents, until such time as the instincts of the parents push them into the gravity-defying act of flight.

In like manner, the Creator endows fish with all of the necessary traits to be at home in the sea or a lake. Fish receive gills, fins, and scales to make their compatibility with their environment complete. Fish do not have to learn to swim. They swim from the moment they are born. Just as the birds fly by doing what comes naturally, so the fish swim.

But then we see the apex of creation, God's crowning creative act, the human species, which alone is made in God's image and given dominion over the birds, the fish, and the whole world. It is the nature of this created being, the human being, to worship God. But something has been added to the mix that causes human beings to act against their natures, to fail to do what comes naturally. We have fallen from our original position in creation, that place wherein, before the fall, Adam and Eve delighted in giving honor, glory, and reverence to their Creator. Since the fall, this natural propensity for worship has been obscured and damaged.

In the first chapter of Romans, the Apostle Paul made it clear that the universal sin, the most foundational sin among human beings, is idolatry. It is the proclivity to exchange the glory of God for a lie, and to worship and serve the creature rather than the ever-blessed Creator. Through the indictment of Romans 1, we learn that all human beings repress the manifest self-disclosure of God and refuse to honor Him as God, "nor [are] thankful" (v. 21). These twin acts of treason against the divine glory, refusing to honor Him as God and refusing to give Him the gratitude that is due Him for all of the blessings we receive from His hand, are so powerful that once a person is converted, these penchants are not instantly or automatically erased. To be sure, the Spirit of God quickens within the souls of the redeemed a new desire for worship. But that desire cannot be left to the natural course of experience. It must be cultivated. It must be learned in accordance with the directives of Scripture. The worship to which we are called in our renewed state is far too important to be left to personal preferences, whims, or marketing strategies. Pleasing God is at the heart of worship. Therefore, our worship must be informed at every point by the Word of God as we seek God's own instructions for worship that is pleasing to Him.

In our time, we have experienced a radical eclipse of God. The shadow that has fallen across the face of God cannot destroy His existence any more than a passing cloud can destroy the sun or the moon. But the eclipse hides the real character of God from His people. It has brought a profound loss of the sense of the holy, and with that, any sense of the gravity and seriousness of godly worship.

We are a people who have lost sight of the threshold and have begun to fail to make a transition on Sunday mornings from the secular to the sacred, from the common to the uncommon, from the profane to the holy. We continue, as did the sons of Aaron, Nadab and Abihu, to offer strange fire before the Lord (Lev. 10:1–2). We have made our worship services more secular than sacred, more common than uncommon, more profane than holy.

This book is a brief introduction to the basic principles of worship, set forth for our instruction and edification, and for our obedience, in Scripture. It looks at both the principles enjoined by Scripture and the models displayed in Scripture. Our modern worship needs the philosophy of the second glance, an ongoing attempt to make sure that all that we do in worship gatherings is to God's glory, to His honor, and according to His will. May this book help bring an end to the eclipse of God in our time, and help us once again render unto God the worship we are designed to give.

CHAPTER 1
THE FORM OF WORSHIP

It was one of those lovely autumn Saturday afternoons when people's thoughts turn to football, golf, or raking leaves. But I was doing something else entirely: reading again the *Discourse on Method and Meditations* of René Descartes.

I appreciate philosophers such as Descartes who pursue the truth by going back to first principles in seeking for foundations upon which everything else is established and from which everything else flows. In my own activity in theology and philosophy, I use this approach frequently, because it is so easy to lose sight of the forest when you get caught among the trees. When I am confused, I like to back up and say: "Okay, what do we know for sure? What is the foundation upon which everything is built?"

That is exactly what I want to do in this study of worship. We are living in a time when there is a manifest crisis of worship in the church. It is almost as if we are in the midst of a rebellion among people who find church less than meaningful. They are bored. They see the experience of Sunday morning as an exercise in irrelevance. As a reaction against that, it seems that almost any church we visit is experimenting with new forms and new patterns of worship. This experimentation has provoked many disputes over the nature of worship.

The worship battle lines tend to be drawn between what is called liturgical worship and nonliturgical worship. In a very real sense, these labels represent a false dilemma. In the first place, any service of worship I have ever attended could be called liturgical. All that *liturgical* means is that there is a liturgy, an order or a pattern, and that certain things are done in the service. The same kind of thing may be said with respect to formal and informal worship. *Informal* simply means "without form." We cannot, however, have corporate worship with no form. There is some form to every worship service, so there is really no such thing as worship that is informal in the literal sense. The issue is not whether we are going to have a liturgy or a form. The question is, "What will be the structure, the style, and the content of the liturgy?"

Once we have settled on a form, we must ask whether it is a legitimate form. To find the answer to that question, we need to return to first principles, to the foundations, and search out what God wants us to do in worship. The issue is not what stimulates or excites us. Though that is not an insignificant or unimportant issue, our overriding concern needs to be what is pleasing to God.

The question we need to ask is this: "If God Himself were to design worship, what would it look like?"

We are not left to speculate on the answer to that question, because vast portions of the Old Testament text are specifically devoted to a style and practice of worship that God Himself ordained and established among His people.

Of course, we cannot go to the Old Testament to discover what is there in terms of the format of worship and then simply carry it across and superimpose it onto the New Testament community. The reason for that is obvious: much of the ritual of the Old Testament focused on the sacrificial system, which was fulfilled once and for all in the atonement of Christ.

Take the rite of circumcision in the Old Testament. When Moses was derelict in circumcising his son, God pursued Moses and threatened to execute him because he had failed to follow God's prescription of giving the sacred rite of circumcision to his children (Exod. 4:24–26). Clearly, then, God regarded circumcision as extremely important. But if I said that we must have our sons circumcised as a religious sign and ritual, I would be under God's condemnation. That is clear from the book of Galatians, where Paul spoke of dealing with those who wanted to insist on total continuity between the Old Testament and the New Testament (Gal. 2). If we follow their lead and insist on total continuity between the testaments, we risk falling into the Judaizing heresy and denying the fulfillment of the covenant that was accomplished by Jesus. Clearly, then, there is some discontinuity between the Old Testament and the New Testament.

However, we must not fall into the trap of thinking that there is no continuity at all between the testaments. The early church passed through a great crisis concerning biblical continuity. This crisis centered on a man named Marcion, who was a "heresiarch," the arch heretic of all time regarding biblical continuity. Marcion taught that the God of the New Testament who is revealed in Jesus is not the same God who appears in the Old Testament. Marcion saw the God of the Old Testament as a tyrannical being, a mean, vengeful, and wrathful God. But the loving Father revealed by Jesus in the New Testament is the true God, Marcion said.

Of course, someone could have pointed out to Marcion that Jesus frequently quoted the Old Testament text and addressed the Old Testament God as His Father. Such passages were indeed problematic for Marcion, so he took his scissors and paste, and altered Scripture so that it conveyed the doctrine he wanted it to convey. He produced an expurgated, or abridged, version of the New Testament. He was the first scholar to offer a formal canon of the New Testament to the church. But it was radically reduced in scope from the New Testament we know today.

The church responded to that heresy by saying, "No, this is not Scripture. This is a truncated version of Scripture." The church did that because it saw the serious danger of looking at the God of the New Testament as alien to the God of the Old Testament. Prompted by the crisis ignited by Marcion's heresy, the church began to formalize the canon of Scripture. In the process, the church affirmed the Scriptural teaching that God is immutable, that His character does not change from generation to generation, from year to year, or from day to day. In other words, the church said that there is continuity from the Old Testament to the New in at least one aspect: God Himself. So, while we have some discontinuity, there is an abiding continuity as well.

I do not know of anyone today who teaches pure, unvarnished Marcionism, but his heresy is alive and well in the evangelical church in our unprecedented neglect of the Old Testament. People, particularly in America, are conditioned to think of Christianity only in terms of the New Testament. I am sure this is why we have a crisis of morality in the church and the pervasive presence of an antinomian theology and behavioral system. Simply put, we have woefully neglected the Old Testament, just as if there is nothing but discontinuity between the two testaments.

An example of this can be seen in our approach to the law of God. Some years ago, I received a letter from a scholar who was upset about some theological issues. He complained because one of my colleagues had charged some other theologians with being antinomian, that is, opposed to the law of God. This man felt an affinity for these other theologians, and he wrote to me because he knew I agreed with the charge of antinomianism. In his letter, this man asked: "How can he charge these men with antinomianism? We are not antinomians. We believe that Christians are responsible to obey all of the commandments of Christ." But then he added, "Of course, we also believe that none of the laws of the Old Testament impose any moral obligation on believers."

I answered him this way: "From now on, I will not discuss or use this term *antinomian* with these other people. Instead of using them as an example, I'll use you, because when you say that the law of God in the Old Testament has no moral obligation on the Christian, you are making the classic expression of what has been defined historically as antinomianism." This man had simply concluded that none of the laws of God in the Old Testament have continuity in the New Testament.

That is one major way we see neglect of the Old Testament; we also see it in worship. We behave as if nothing God said on the subject of worship in the Old Testament applies today. If we are to come back to the foundation, if we are to please God in our worship, does it not make sense to ask whether there has ever been a time when the unchanging God Himself revealed the kind of worship that was pleasing to Him? I believe that the answer is yes, and I believe that there was such a time.

When we affirm the inerrancy of Scripture, we are often charged with holding a view of inspiration that teaches a dictation theory of inspiration. Of course, historic orthodoxy does not teach such a view. The church has never taught that God dictated every word of, for example, the book of Romans, with Paul acting as a secretary and simply recording the words God dictated from heaven. Conservative theologians actually bend over backward to show that the mode of inspiration is not expressed in terms of dictation.

However, if there ever was a time when God dictated revelation, it was in those passages in the Pentateuch where He told the people word for word, line upon line, precept upon precept how He wanted Old Testament worship to be conducted. He told the Israelites how the tabernacle was to be built. He gave detailed instructions for the ephod and the garments of the priests. He laid down specific laws governing the behavior of the priests and the people in and around the sanctuary. He outlined the services, the offerings, and the festivals. In other words, God took great pains to be very specific about the form of worship in Israel.

Yes, there is discontinuity. We do not have a temple now. The curtain of the Holy of Holies has been torn. We do not make offerings on the altar of sacrifice today. But there is continuity, too. I believe we can discern principles in the patterns of worship that God revealed from heaven to His people in the Old Testament, and that those principles can and should inform the patterns our worship follows.

We must be careful, however, as we dig into these Old Testament passages in upcoming chapters, that we do not allow the pursuit of proper form in worship to become an end in itself. That has been the case far too often in the history of God's people, from ancient Israel to Jesus's time to the Reformation, with sad results in each instance.

People use various adjectives to differentiate styles of worship. Some speak of high liturgy or low liturgy, or they speak of formal worship in relative degrees, depending on whether the ministers or priests wear vestments, whether printed prayers or spontaneous prayers are used, whether the music is classical or contemporary, and other criteria. These adjectives are employed because different styles of worship have arisen as a reaction against what could be called a high liturgy or a classical, traditional pattern of worship. Why has that reaction occurred?

At the time of the Reformation, some people in Protestant churches reacted against the traditional Roman Catholic style of worship. Some of that reaction was theological, but not all of it. Some of it was based on a zealous desire to do nothing in the way Rome did it. For instance, during the time Martin Luther hid at Wartburg Castle and translated the Bible from the original languages into German, one of his disciples in Wittenberg, Andreas Carlstadt, started vandalizing churches, smashing stained-glass windows, overturning the furniture, and doing all sorts of damage in the name of reform. When Luther heard of this, he was upset and disciplined Carlstadt for his overzealous reaction against the sacred things of the past.

Carlstadt erroneously directed his ire against the "form" of Roman Catholic worship. The problem was not with the form but with the formalism into which Rome had fallen. The word *formalism* means that the form becomes the end in itself. Another word that means much the same is *externalism*, which is the condition that happens when all that exists are the external elements, while the internal elements, the heart and soul, are absent. The Reformers' true goal was to cure the formalism and externalism of the Roman Catholic Church. In the same way, the Old Testament prophets were vehement in their denunciations of the dead, empty formalism into which Jewish worship had degenerated.

As a seminary student, I had to read two books on worship, one that favored a low liturgy and another that favored a high liturgy. The book that favored the low liturgy was presented as an expression of "prophetic" worship in the church, whereas the book that advocated a high liturgy presented itself as following the priestly tradition of worship. After reading these books, we students had to defend one or the other style of worship. I was astonished to discover that I was the only person in the class who favored the high liturgy and the priestly tradition. My professor was equally surprised at me, because he knew that I was a committed evangelical Christian, and evangelicals traditionally shy away from liturgical worship.

Why did I choose the high liturgy position? The author of the book on the priestly tradition convinced me by showing that when we go back to the prophetic critique of the deadly forms of worship that God rejected in Israel, the prophets were reformers but not revolutionaries. What is the difference? The prophets nowhere rejected the liturgies of worship that God had ordained for His people. Instead, the prophets denounced the decadence of the people's practice in following these liturgies. The problem was not with the liturgies; the problem was with the worshippers who came with cold hearts and went through the liturgies simply by rote, with uninvolved and untouched hearts.

Jesus, too, was a reformer in this sense. Exhibit A of externalism in the Bible is the Pharisees, who went through all of the outward rites, all of the liturgies that God had prescribed, but their hearts were not in it. They skated on the surface of superficial lip service to God. Jesus said this of them: "Hypocrites! Well did Isaiah prophesy about you, saying: 'These people draw near to Me with their mouth, and honor Me with their lips, but their heart is far from Me. And in vain they worship Me'" (Matt. 15:7–9a).

There is no doubt that God wants His worship to have form, so the question is not whether we should have a liturgy or not. The issue is whether the liturgy is biblical in its content and, ultimately, whether we are using the liturgy to worship in spirit and in truth. No matter what the liturgy is, whether it is plain and simple or high and complex, it can be formalized and externalized so that it is corrupted to the point that God despises it. As we seek out the forms of worship that please God, we must be vigilant lest we fall into formalism or externalism.

CHAPTER 2
SACRIFICES IN FAITH

The most common word for worship in the Greek New Testament is familiar to us in our own term for false worship. The word *idolatry*, which means "the worship of idols," is simply a combination of the word *idol* and the Greek word *latria*. But in the New Testament, *latria* is the word that is translated most frequently as "worship" in its proper, positive sense.

The concept of worship embodied in the word *latria* is found very early in the Old Testament and throughout the history of the Jews. According to scholars, the term originally referred to a particular service that people rendered with a view to gaining some kind of reward or compensation on an earthly scale. However, it was used in the Greek translation of the Old Testament almost exclusively with reference to cultic service. When I use the term *cultic*, I am not referring to cults or to the occult but to the *cultus*, which was the center of worship, the behavior that was focused in and around the tabernacle or the temple in the Old Testament. Cultic service encompassed the liturgical and ritual behavior of the Jews in the Old Testament. And so, the term *latria* referred to the practices of worship in the religious life of Israel.

There were three basic components of this concept of *latria* in the Jewish nation. They were the offering of praise to God, the offering of prayer to God, and the offering of sacrifice to God. In other words, worship in Israel was understood basically in terms of praise, prayer, and the offering of sacrifices. Of the three, the component that was most central to Old Testament worship was the third, the offering of sacrifices. In fact, we can reduce Old Testament worship to a single, central focus—going to the tabernacle or the temple to offer sacrifices. Even praise and prayer were spiritual forms of sacrifice. That was why, in the elaborate tabernacle and temple, God ordained that there should be an altar of incense where the prayers of the saints were symbolically offered up to God as sacrifices.

I stress this because we live in the New Testament era and we realize that the sacrifice that Christ offered as our High Priest in the atonement, the offering up of Himself as the supreme sacrifice to God, fulfilled all the symbolism and ritual of Old Testament worship. His was the quintessential sacrifice, given on our behalf. For this reason, we do not go to church and put bulls, sheep, goats, or anything else on an altar as burnt offerings to the Lord. But because we do not offer sacrifices of the type and form that were customary in the Old Testament, I am afraid we have lost sight of this central, essential dimension of what worship is about historically.

As we look at worship, I want to go back to the roots. Let us see how God ordained worship in the first place, what were its constituent elements, and how the Old Testament worship of Israel, though fulfilled in the ultimate act of sacrifice by Christ on the cross, nevertheless is to inform our worship today. Our understanding of worship is truncated if we see it completely apart from its Old Testament origins.

There is no question of the importance of sacrifice in the ancient Israelite *cultus*. Vast sections of the five books of Moses describe in great detail the various sacrifices God commanded for His people. But the importance of sacrifice in worship was clear long before God gave His law.

In the middle of the twentieth century, a French Roman Catholic theologian named Yves Congar published an essay titled *Ecclesia ab Abel*; that is, *The Church from Abel*. In that work, Congar indicated that the church did not begin in the New Testament; in reality, it began as soon as creation was established, and worship took place among the original creatures God made. I would have titled the essay *Ecclesia ab Adam*, or *The Church from Adam*, because I believe the concept of the church can be traced even further back to Abel's father and mother, who enjoyed fellowship in the immediate presence of God that certainly included worship. But Congar started his study of the church not with Adam and Eve but with Abel because of the record that we have in the early chapters of Genesis of the first forms of liturgy or worship.

Let us go back to the beginning, or at least to the beginning of the reconstituted church of God after the fall. I am not going to the garden of Eden, where worship was uninhibited, without any intervening failures that would disrupt in any way the naked, immediate fellowship that Adam and Eve enjoyed in the presence of God. I am going instead to Genesis 4, where we read:

> Now Adam knew Eve his wife, and she conceived and bore Cain, and said, "I have acquired a man from the LORD." Then she bore again, this time his brother Abel. Now Abel was a keeper of sheep, but Cain was a tiller of the ground. And in the process of time it came to pass that Cain brought an offering of the fruit of the ground to the LORD. Abel also brought of the firstborn of his flock and of their fat. And the LORD respected Abel and his offering, but He did not respect Cain and his offering. And Cain was very angry, and his countenance fell. (vv. 1–5)

This narrative of the first act of the *cultus* of Israel is so brief and sketchy that it has provoked much speculation. We are not told very much about these two, only that they were brothers. Some believe the text implies that they were twins, but that is debated. What we know is that Cain was the firstborn, and that is very important from a Jewish perspective. In the ancient world, through the patristic period and all the way through the Old Testament, the firstborn son was the one who inherited the birthright and received the office of honor and distinction in the home. That custom did not begin with Jacob and Esau; it was already operative in the family of Adam and Eve. Their firstborn son was Cain and their second born was Abel. So, in terms of familial status, the glory went to Cain, not to Abel.

This text also shows there was a division of labor between Cain and Abel. They had different vocations, different functions to perform. One raised produce from the earth, and the other was a shepherd. The higher of the two roles in terms of dignity, respect, and status in the family was given to the firstborn, Cain, who was given the responsibility to sow the seed for the harvest. Abel's role was of a lower significance. In fact, the job of shepherding has always held very little status in Israel; this was so even in Jesus's time. Shepherds were not even allowed to give testimony in court because they were considered utterly untrustworthy, the dregs of society. In other words, the shepherd was seen as just a bit above a slave. He was a lowly servant. That is why it was so significant that the first announcement of the birth of Jesus was given to shepherds in the fields outside Bethlehem. Those shepherds had the lowest status in the culture of that time. Things were much the same in the time of the first family, and that is significant to what occurred in Genesis 4.

When the moment came for worship, the men brought different kinds of offerings for their sacrifices to God. One brought fruits and vegetables. The other brought an animal from the flock and its fat. Even though Cain was the firstborn and had the more honored job, God "respected," or accepted, Abel's offering but not Cain's. Why was that? The usual answer is that Abel's offering, an animal, was superior substantially, in terms of its content. Many people are led to this conclusion because, in the sacrificial system of the Old Testament, the sacrifice God normally required was a lamb. Yet, some exceptions were made. For example, when Mary and Joseph first presented Jesus at the temple, Mary gave an offering of two pigeons (Luke 2:22–24). That was allowed by Jewish law, but only in the case of extreme poverty. In most cases, a lamb was sacrificed. However, while the Old Testament specified that the sacrifice must be of the highest quality—a lamb without blemish—God never said that a sacrifice of the firstfruits of the flock was intrinsically superior to a sacrifice of the firstfruits of the harvest.

I labor this point because, throughout history, in literature, sermons, and expositions, theologians have jumped to the conclusion that God respected Abel's sacrifice and did not respect Cain's because Abel brought an animal, a living creature, and Cain brought produce from the field. However, that difference had absolutely nothing to do with the variance of God's response to the two sacrifices. Martin Luther, I think rightly, remarked that Abel could have sacrificed the shell of a nut and it would have been more pleasing to God than the sacrifice brought by Cain. That was because it was not *what* Abel offered to God but *how* he offered it that made the difference.

The all-encompassing criterion for acceptable sacrifice before God in the Old Testament was the posture and the attitude of the person making the sacrifice. Jesus affirmed this truth when He watched worshippers making their offerings in the temple (Mark 12:41–44). He pronounced His benediction on the widow who offered her two mites, the smallest measure of currency. Jesus pointed out that her gift was more costly for her than the offerings of the men of great wealth, who dropped the equivalent of $10,000 into the offering plate. He said that because He was able to read her heart when she gave her sacrifice. The rich men gave because they wanted the applause of men or some honor in the sight of God, but Jesus knew the poor widow had a different motive.

The Apostle Paul told us that the Lord "loves a cheerful giver" (2 Cor. 9:7). We hear that verse so often we can become jaded to it and not take the time to think about what it means. Paul was not saying God loves just anyone who gives. After all, Cain gave, but God was not pleased with him at all. No, Paul declared that God loves a particular kind of giver, a cheerful giver. The term *cheerful* describes the disposition of the heart, the attitude of the soul in the giving of the gift.

Imagine that it is Sunday morning, and the ushers come to receive our offering, and suppose we are thinking: "Here they come again with their hands out, asking for tithes and offerings, and people are watching to see if I am going to put anything in the plate. I'll give it because it is my duty to tithe." We might as well keep our tithe money in our pockets, because according to the Scriptures, those kinds of sacrifices are loathsome to God. But He delights in those who bring their gifts with joy as an act of worship.

How do we know that Cain and Abel came to make their offerings with different heart dispositions? Am I reading between the lines, speculating about the Old Testament text, and imposing basic principles from the rest of the Old Testament upon this passage that is so mute in its extension? No, we know this because the Word of God clearly states that Abel made his sacrifice with a different attitude.

In Hebrews 11, we find the roll call of the saints, commemorating the heroic and glorious activities of the people of God throughout church history. There were those who, for the cause of righteousness and for the faith, were sawed in two, fed to wild beasts, murdered, stoned, despised, hated, and ridiculed. But God was pleased because they were faithful. The litany goes on and on: "By faith Abraham.... By faith Isaac.... By faith Jacob.... By faith Moses...." And right there, among these great heroes of the faith, stands Abel: "By faith Abel offered to God a more excellent sacrifice than Cain" (v. 4). Abel's faith made all the difference.

What did it mean for Abel to offer a sacrifice in faith? Now I am going to speculate, because the gaps in the biblical history are not filled in.

The promise of our redemption was first announced to Adam and Eve after they sinned and violated their moral relationship with God. God gave them the *protoevangelium*, the original announcement of the gospel: The Seed of the woman would crush the head of the Serpent, and in the process He would be wounded in His heel (Gen. 3:15). If that verse were the only reference to redemption in the Bible, no one could penetrate its meaning because it is so cryptic. However, since we have the benefit of the unveiling of God's plan of redemption through the ages and through the Scriptures, we know exactly to what God was referring in Genesis 3:15. In that promise, the gospel was given to Adam and Eve, the gospel of forgiveness, restoration, and fellowship with God. It was the gospel that proclaims the crushing of the Evil One, who disrupts and mars the beauty and holiness of God's creation. God promised that the Evil One would be destroyed by the sacrifice of the woman's Seed, who would be wounded in the process of His conquest. This promise of the sacrifice of the Seed of the woman was central to Abel's worship. The irony is that this first gospel was given in the context of the cursing of the Serpent after the fall.

The worship of God has always involved the spoken word of promise, and from the very beginning, God often added to the word some kind of tangible, sensory sign. He said to Noah: "I will never destroy the world again by a flood. Look in the sky, Noah. I have set My bow in the sky" (see Gen. 9:13–16). He said to Abraham: "Behold, I will make you the father of a great nation, and your seed will be like the stars in the sky and like the sand on the seashore. And this will be a sign to you and to all generations, the sign of circumcision" (see Gen. 17:1–14; 22:17). In these and other instances, the word of promise was supported by a tangible sign.

In general terms, the word of promise throughout every page of the Old Testament is the promise of the coming Redeemer, who would save His people from their sins by offering a perfect sacrifice. From the very beginning, redemption was tied to sacrifice. That is why the dramatic reinforcement of the word of promise throughout the Old Testament is an elaborate ritual that focuses on sacrifice. This did not start with Moses. We see it here in Genesis 4, where Abel came with a sacrifice of faith.

Why did he do it? When it came time to worship God, why did Abel seek to worship by means of a sacrifice? Obviously this kind of worship was instituted and ordained by God Himself.

My speculation is this: I cannot imagine that our first parents did not explain to their sons the hope that sustained them. That hope was the most important promise that Adam and Eve had received, the promise that the Seed of the woman would crush the head of the Serpent at the cost of the wounding of His heel. How many hours do you suppose Adam and Eve sat with their children, preaching the gospel to them and teaching them the elements of appropriate worship?

However, it was not enough for Cain and Abel to merely hear Adam and Eve speak of the promise. The issue was whether they would trust the promise. What would they trust in ultimately to reconcile them to the Father? What would they trust in to receive the blessing of God?

There is no need to speculate about what Cain was trusting when he brought his offering. Throughout the history of Israel, one heresy was perpetuated from one family to the next, and even Jesus had to combat it in His dealings with the rabbis of His time. It was lineage. This was the view that led many to say to themselves: "I am the firstborn, so my future rests in my superior status as the elder son. I'll go to church and go through the rituals like everyone else does. I'll bring my produce. I'll drop it in the collection plate. But my confidence is in my status, in my lineage."

We can almost hear God saying to Cain, "Cain, Cain, if you trust in yourself in any way, in your family position, in your own strength, in your skill as a farmer or any works that you are able to perform, even in your own faith—I have no respect for that. Your worship is an abomination to Me. But your brother has nothing of this world upon which to rely. He is a servant; he is a shepherd. He is a sinner who knows he cannot save himself, and when he comes into My house, he comes trusting My mercy, trusting My word, trusting My promise alone. I love his sacrifice because I love him. I love him because he is righteous. But you are not. Your father taught you that the only way you can be righteous in My sight is by faith."

David knew what Cain did not: "For You do not desire sacrifice, or else I would give it; You do not delight in burnt offering. The sacrifices of God are a broken spirit, a broken and a contrite heart—these, O God, You will not despise" (Ps. 51:16–17). And Jesus explained the essence of worship to the woman of Sychar: "But the hour is coming, and now is, when the true worshipers will worship the Father in spirit and truth" (John 4:23). Notice that "in spirit" comes first. There is some ambiguity about that text, but the basic thrust of it is that God looks on the spiritual attitude of the person who comes before Him to worship. So, true worship—true *latria*, true sacrifice, true service—begins in the soul.

I once knew a man who was young in the faith and full of the enthusiasm so characteristic of those who are newly born-again. He was in love with the Word of God, studying the Scriptures intently every day. I cannot remember ever seeing a young Christian who set his heart so diligently on the pursuit of the knowledge of God. He came to me one day and said: "Romans eight and nine—this is the most exciting thing I have read yet. You know, 'Jacob have I loved, Esau have I hated'—election and all that. It all makes so much sense. I know that is the only way I could get in." He was delirious in his excitement about one of the most controversial doctrines of the Christian faith. As I listened to him gushing with joy over Romans 8 and 9, I was thinking, "If you love this, you have to be born-again." But at the same time, I thought that most people who read that portion of Scripture react with indignation, anger, hostility, and resistance.

That was Cain's reaction to the word of God. Genesis 4 says that when God did not respect his offering, he became irate and his countenance fell. We know what righteous indignation is. We associate that with the wrath of God. When God is angry, it is a holy anger, a righteous anger. No one can ever accuse God of being unfairly, unjustly, or arbitrarily angry. People get angry with others, sometimes justly, sometimes unjustly. At times they impute wrong motives to each other. They do not have all the facts they need; if they knew more, they would not be angry. We have all had experiences like that. But if God is angry with us, there are no mitigating circumstances. We cannot say to God, "God, if You only knew all of the facts, You would not be angry with me." It was presumptuous of Cain to be angry when God did not respect his offering. Perhaps nothing proves more vividly the state of Cain's heart than his reaction to God's judgment.

If we are children of Christ and we stand before the judgment seat of God on the last day and God says to us, "You're covered by the blood of My Son, and it is a good thing, because you did this, this, this, this, and this," we will not say, "But, Lord, I did this in Your name; I did that in Your name. You really are not being fair." However, there will be many who will respond in just that manner. Jesus is going to say to those people, "Please leave, I do not know who you are" (see Matt. 25). A person who trusts God trusts not only His promises but also His judgment. Even in a prayer of contrition, such a person acknowledges that God would be absolutely justified to destroy him for his sin. You can never come to God's church or to the Lord's Table thinking that God owes you something. If you do, you are better off not to pray, not to commune, because you are blaspheming and slandering the Giver of every good and perfect gift, who has treated you only with mercy.

Unlike Cain, Abel was humble in his worship, which is the only possible posture for a fallen human being to have in the context of worship. Arrogant worship is an oxymoron, a contradiction in terms. Yet we see it throughout Scripture. The gospel was given to Adam and Eve. As redemptive history unfolded, the people of Israel continued to recite the promise and to demonstrate it with their liturgy, their signs, their sacraments, and their cultic worship. But the judgment of the prophets that came upon the house of Israel was this: "Your worship has become *idololatria*. You are not putting your faith in God; you are putting it in Baal, in the temple, in the rituals you are doing, in your heritage, in your biology. You are trusting in everything else but God."

Have you ever wondered why there is a universal phenomenon of religion? You can go anywhere on the globe and find evidence of cultic practices of sacrifice. Why is that? I suggest that it is because the original program and prescription for the worship of the living God were sacrifice. Adam told it to Cain, Abel, and Seth. Seth told it to Enoch, and he told it to his sons and they to their sons and so on. It was taught to Abraham. It was taught to Isaac. It was taught to Jacob. It was taught to Joseph. It was taught to Moses. It was also taught to Ishmael and to Esau, and so the idea of the requirement of sacrifice in faith pervaded the whole human race.

But today the need for sacrifices to be made in faith is forgotten—we hear that it does not matter what you believe as long as you are sincere. In fact, the basic requirement of sacrifice is unknown—it does not matter what your religious practices are. It does not matter what you worship. It only matters that you do worship. It is said that the Jews worship God in their way, the Muslims worship God in their way, and the Buddhists worship in their way. The unspoken assumption is that God is willing to receive, honor, and respect any kind of worship that people bring.

God did not respect all of the worship in Genesis 4. He had no respect for Cain's worship. And Cain responded in anger when he saw that his worship was unacceptable to God. A faithful person, a righteous person, would have said, "Oh, my God. I am heartily sorry for having sinned against You. Teach me Your statutes, Oh Lord. Show me the more excellent way. Change my heart, so that the offering that I bring You next Sabbath day will honor you. I am glad, at least, Holy Father, that You were pleased with my brother's offering. Father, give me an attitude by which I can learn from my brother, because my brother lives by faith and is trying to obey You." But that was not Cain's response.

In reality, that is never the response of the godless to the godly. Which of the prophets did they not kill? Which of the reformers in church history was not despised by the organized church? Like Cain, who rose up and slew his brother Abel, wicked churches have spilled the blood of true Christians. In fact, it was the church that rose up to kill Jesus because He did not respect their sacrifices.

I have never been tortured or put on trial for my faith. The persecution I have had to endure in this world is minuscule compared to what the heroes of the faith went through. But whatever persecution I have known in my life, the heaviest weight of it has come from the false church, that part of the church that does not believe the gospel and has no heart for worship. The church has always been composed of wheat and tares, and the first church was no exception. The tares (Cain) were very religious, but they hated God, and they hated the wheat as well. So, they moved to destroy the wheat (Abel). We need to know that because it has always been so.

Remember the word Jesus used repeatedly for the religious leaders of His day: *hypocrite*. He said, "You make your sacrifices; you pay your tithes; you read your Bible. But woe unto you scribes and

Pharisees, hypocrites. You're playacting. There is no faith in your hearts. You're not offering Me worship in faith." They were very religious, but their hearts were far from God.

The single most important thing to understand about worship is that the only worship acceptable to God is worship proceeding from a heart that is trusting in God, and in God alone.

CHAPTER 3
LIVING SACRIFICES

I once wrote a book on human dignity. In that book, I mentioned an exercise a consultant once showed me. He said, "This is going to be a fun exercise, R. C. I want you to write down the five most meaningful compliments people have given you in your lifetime." He was right—it was a fun exercise. I did not have to think about the criticisms or the insults that I had had to deal with in my life; rather, I was able to focus on the nice things people had said to me.

As I thought about those compliments and wrote down the five that seemed most significant, I was astonished to see that every one of the things I listed—comments that had come from people's mouths—had occurred before I was twenty-one years of age, and yet I could remember them years and years later. Then the consultant began to show me that these comments had had a tremendously important shaping influence on my life. He also indicated to me that the people who gave these compliments were individuals whose judgment I valued and whose words I cherished because they were authority figures in my life: coaches, relatives, teachers, and so forth. In fact, two of the five compliments I listed were from my eighth-grade English teacher, and I suddenly began to realize what a tremendous influence that woman had had in my life.

As we discussed these things, the consultant pointed out to me that there must have been times when people had said even nicer things about me. He asked, "Has not anyone ever given you a higher compliment than the ones that you've put down in this list?"

"Well, yes," I said, and I mentioned a couple that came to mind.

"Why didn't you write those down on the paper?" he asked.

"That's easy," I said with a smile. "I didn't write them down because I didn't believe them."

I judged those particular compliments to be insincere. They were flattery, and I intuitively understood the difference between flattery and a genuine compliment. We somehow tend to know when people are giving us empty words of praise, of flattery, words that are not sincere. We all have received praise that is not sincere, and there is something insulting about it. The very hollowness of it torments us in a way. We would like to be able to believe all the nice things people say about us—even when we know they do not mean what they are saying.

God's feelings are not hurt by insincere praise, but neither is He honored by it. God is never honored by flattery. That is why true worship must be sincere.

In the previous chapter, we saw that sacrifice was the central element of Old Testament worship. We saw that this emphasis on sacrifice can be traced back to Cain and Abel, and that God was pleased with Abel's sacrifice but that He rejected Cain's. The difference was that Abel worshipped from a heart that was trusting in God alone.

The sacrifices that were made in the Old Testament were to be sacrifices of praise, and praise is an attempt to express honor. The central element of worship in the Bible involved honoring, blessing, esteeming, and reverencing God. A sacrifice was offered as an outward sign of a heart that was filled with awe, reverence, and respect toward God. When a sacrifice was not given in faith, it was nothing more than an external rite, a formal pattern of behavior that was not an expression of true faith that held God in the highest possible esteem and reverence. It lacked what the Wisdom Literature calls the fear of the Lord, that sense of awe by which the heart is inclined to adore and to honor the Creator. The very heart of worship, as the Bible makes clear, is the business of expressing, from the depths of our spirits, the highest possible honor we can offer before God.

Abel sincerely wanted to honor God in his worship, but Cain was not interested in honoring God. Clearly, the honor that is expressed toward God in worship may be insincere.

When Jesus encountered the Samaritan woman at the well in Sychar, she engaged Him in a theological debate, using it as a diversion from her personal guilt, which Jesus had exposed. She asked Jesus a question about worship, saying, "The fathers of our people—that is, the Samaritans—said we should worship God here at Mount Gerizim. That is our traditional site, but you Jews worship God in

Jerusalem. Now, where is it that we are supposed to worship?" In effect, Jesus replied, "The time is coming and now is when you will not worship the Father either in Mount Gerizim or in Jerusalem, but the Father is seeking those who will worship Him in spirit and in truth" (see John 4:20–24).

That statement by Jesus was profound. What did He mean? He was not saying that God used to be localized in a single central sanctuary—the tabernacle or the temple, Mount Gerizim or Jerusalem—but now His people could worship Him anywhere. That was not the point. Rather, Jesus was addressing the Samaritan woman's superficial understanding of what worship was and always has been. It was not about the location or the substance of the sacrifice, such as whether it was an animal sacrifice or a cereal sacrifice. Rather, Jesus was talking about the nature of the worship that is offered to God. Genuine worship is spiritual and true. That was what God wanted then, and that is what He is looking for today.

Christ manifested and demonstrated that sort of worship in His own life. When Jesus walked through Samaria, every minute He was there, He gave the Father the sacrifice of praise. In other words, the spirit of Christ worshipped the Father in truth. When He came to Jerusalem, the Son of God adored the Father in spirit and in truth; when He was in Capernaum, He gave the sacrifice of praise perfectly. It did not matter where He was, He was always authentic in the honor He bestowed upon His Father.

In order to come to a New Testament definition of true spiritual worship, the kind of worship that is pleasing to God, we have to turn our attention to Paul's letter to the church at Rome. Commentators on Romans usually divide the book between the first eleven chapters and the final five. In the first eleven chapters, Paul gave his greatest exposition of the drama of redemption, of the person and work of Christ, of God's gracious election, and of the way in which He justifies sinners by His mercy and grace. Beginning in the twelfth chapter, there is a clear and decisive shift in the Apostle's language and style. Paul moved from the exposition of the content of the gospel to what we can call the practical application of it.

Romans 12 begins with an Apostolic entreaty. Paul started the chapter with these words: "I beseech you." These are words of passion. Paul was not just saying, "I commend to you," or "I would like to instruct you," or "Please give your attention to this." He was engaged in a passionate act. He was saying to his readers, "I beg of you …"

Then Paul added the critical word *therefore*. In Scripture, the term *therefore* always introduces a conclusion that flows out of, and results from, a previous argument. Before we look at Paul's conclusion, let's consider the argument on which it is based.

We could look at the "therefore" in Romans 12:1 in light of what he has said in chapter 11, and that is certainly a legitimate possibility in terms of the syntax. But this "therefore" also could be referring to everything that has come before it. Given the clear line of division between the content emphasis of the first eleven chapters and the final five, I am inclined to think that this "therefore" is introducing a conclusion based on everything that has come up to this point in the epistle. I hear the Apostle saying this: "In light of God's revelation of that righteousness that is made available to us by faith, in light of God's grace of election, in light of all of the gospel, I come to you Romans now begging for something that should flow out of the gospel by irresistible logic."

What was that thing for which the Apostle was begging? Paul wrote, "I beseech you therefore, brethren, by the mercies of God, that you present your bodies a living sacrifice, holy, acceptable to God, which is your reasonable service" (v. 1). Some other translations render this a little differently. They include the entreaty and the word *therefore*, but instead of saying, "I beseech you to present your bodies a living sacrifice," they render it this way: "I beg you to present yourselves as a living sacrifice, a sacrifice that is holy, that is sacred, a sacrifice that is acceptable to God." Instead of translating the last clause as "which is your reasonable service," they translate it with these words: "which is your spiritual worship." This captures the essence of worship as it is understood in light of the gospel.

We no longer go to the sanctuary and sprinkle the blood of bulls and goats upon an altar. However, we still give gifts to God. We still bring our tithes and our offerings to Him as part of our outward expression of commitment to Him. But we remember David's words in his penitential psalm: "For You do not desire sacrifice, or else would I give it; You do not delight in burnt offering. The sacrifices of God are a broken spirit, a broken and a contrite heart—these, O God, You will not despise" (Ps. 51:16–17). David understood what Abel understood but what never occurred to Cain: that the sacrifice God accepts, the one that pleases Him, is one that is not made unholy by a selfish motivation or a dishonest charade, but a sacrifice that comes from the heart.

It is as if Paul said to the Romans: "Think of the gospel. What is your response to what Christ has done for you—Christ, who spared nothing, who gave His life for His people, who made the ultimate sacrifice for His sheep? How do we respond to that? What is the reasonable response?" Paul said, "Here is your reasonable service or your spiritual worship."

So, we are to respond to the gospel with a sacrifice—not a sacrifice of money, of time, or of material goods, but a sacrifice of our lives. Paul said we are to present to God our bodies—that is, ourselves—as living sacrifices. Abel's sacrifice was acceptable to God when he offered an animal; but it was a dead sacrifice. Paul was saying that, in light of the gospel, God wants a living sacrifice. He is not asking for martyrdom or for us to give our blood. He wants something more. He wants our lives. The response of faith is a giving of oneself, body and soul, to Christ.

In the first few weeks of my Christian life after my conversion in 1957, I heard a certain gospel hymn for the first time. It was called "Where He Leads Me, I Will Follow." It says, "I can hear my Savior calling." The song suggests that our response to Christ's call should be the response of the disciples, who left everything to follow Him. That made sense to me. I understood, even in the first two weeks of my Christian experience, that God plays for keeps. He wants our hearts, our souls, our lives. He wants us to make the seeking of His kingdom the main and central business of our lives. He does not want us to play with religion, to dabble in church, or to simply write a check. He wants us—body and soul.

I have not given that sacrifice. I have never given my whole self to God or given my reasonable service to Him. I have failed in my spiritual duty. And yet, that is what worship is—the presenting of ourselves on the altar of praise, so that what we think, what we do, and how we live is motivated by a desire to honor God. I wish I could say to God on the judgment day, "Oh, God, everything I did was done out of a desire to honor You." But I had better not stand before Him and say that, because if I do I know what He would say back. He would tell me that every sacrifice I have ever offered has been marred, sullied, and compromised by the sin I have brought with it. If He were to look at the sacrifice that I offered, even if I offered it in the name of Christ, He would reject it as radically as He rejected the offering of Cain. My only hope is the glorious truth that the offering I give to my Creator today is carried to His presence by the perfect Mediator, who takes our sacrifices of praise and presents them to the Father.

Paul said, "I beseech you therefore, brethren, by the mercies of God, that you present your bodies a living sacrifice, holy, acceptable to God, which is your reasonable service" (Rom. 12:1). The sacrifice of our lives to God is the only reasonable response to the One who has paid such a high cost for our redemption. Only in this way can we sincerely honor the one true God.

CHAPTER 4
THE HOUSE OF PRAYER

When my wife, Vesta, and I were engaged, we liked to find a place to pray together after going out on a date. However, the only church in our community that was unlocked at night so that people could go in and pray was the Roman Catholic church. That bothered me, so I went to our pastor at the Presbyterian church and asked why we could not go into the church to pray. He said that the insurance premiums required that the church be locked.

That struck me as odd. The Roman Catholic church was more ornate and had more expensive items all around the sanctuary. It seemed that the Roman Catholic church had a whole lot more to lose than the Protestant churches, and yet the Roman Catholic sanctuary was kept open.

The reason for the difference is simple. It is an integral part of Roman Catholic devotion for people to see the church building as a sanctuary for prayer. That is not the case with Protestants. When I was in seminary, I could not find people to pray with, so I went to Duquesne University each week, to the convent of the mother house of the Mission Helpers of the Sacred Heart, an order of nuns that was involved in mission work to people who were sick and had other needs. I met with the nuns in their chapel and prayed with them, because prayer was part of their routine.

We could get into the theology of all that is involved in the Roman Catholic practice of prayer, but that is not the point. The point is that Roman Catholics go to their sanctuaries at all times of the day to pray. You can scarcely walk into the sanctuary of a large Roman Catholic church and find it vacant. At almost any hour, there will be people sitting in the pews or over in some little alcove where the candles are, and they will be praying.

In chapter 2, I noted that there were three basic components of the worship practices of ancient Israel: the offering of praise, prayer, and sacrifice to God. Of the three, sacrifice was the most crucial element because Jewish worship centered on going to the tabernacle or the temple to offer sacrifices. We saw that even praise and prayer were spiritual forms of sacrifice. For this reason, we have looked at the role of sacrifice in worship then and now in the last two chapters.

We also noted that God ordained that there should be a second altar in the tabernacle and temple, in addition to the altar of burnt offering. This was the altar of incense. God described it for His people in detail in Exodus 30:1–9:

> You shall make an altar to burn incense on; you shall make it of acacia wood. A cubit shall be its length and a cubit its width—it shall be square—and two cubits shall be its height. Its horns shall be of one piece with it. And you shall overlay its top, its sides all around, and its horns with pure gold; and you shall make for it a molding of gold all around. Two gold rings you shall make for it, under the molding on both its sides.... You shall make the poles of acacia wood, and overlay them with gold. And you shall put it before the veil that is before the ark of the Testimony, before the mercy seat that is over the Testimony, where I will meet with you.
>
> Aaron shall burn on it sweet incense every morning; when he tends the lamps, he shall burn incense on it. And when Aaron lights the lamps at twilight, he shall burn incense on it, a perpetual incense before the LORD throughout your generations. You shall not offer strange incense on it, or a burnt offering, or a grain offering; nor shall you pour a drink offering on it.

In short, God wanted one altar set aside for a unique purpose. God said: "I do not want cereal offerings on it. I do not want meat offerings on it. I do not want oblations poured across it. This is to be a perpetual offering to God every single day."

Why did God want incense to be burned constantly in His sanctuary? Incense has much symbolism in Scripture, but one major factor is that the rising smoke of the incense was symbolic of the prayers of God's people ascending to His throne (Rev. 5:8; 8:3–4). In commanding the perpetual burning of incense, God was telling His people they were not to draw near to Him except in an attitude of prayer. That was the principle. So, prayer was a very significant element of the ancient Israelite *cultus*.

Perhaps the clearest picture of the place of prayer as God ordained it for Israelite worship occurs not in the Old Testament but in the New Testament book of Luke. Beginning in Luke 1:5, we read: "There was in the days of Herod, the king of Judea, a certain priest named Zacharias, of the division of Abijah. His wife was of the daughters of Aaron, and her name was Elizabeth."

It is interesting that Luke began his book with the story of a man who was a priest and a woman who was the wife of a priest and the daughter of a priest. For Luke, this was how the gospel began. He continued:

> And they were both righteous before God, walking in all the commandments and ordinances of the Lord blameless. But they had no child, because Elizabeth was barren, and they were both well advanced in years.
>
> So it was, that while he was serving as priest before God in the order of his division, according to the custom of the priesthood, his lot fell to burn incense when he went into the temple of the Lord. And the whole multitude of the people was praying outside at the hour of incense. (Luke 1:6–10)

There were roughly seven thousand to eight thousand priests in Israel, and only a handful of them served in the temple in Jerusalem. The rest of them were like parish priests today; they were out in the villages, performing their services. The dream of each one of those village priests was to participate someday in the liturgy of the temple. However, there were only a couple of times in the year when that opportunity presented itself, so priests were selected for the various temple tasks by lot. It was mathematically probable that a village priest would go his whole life and never win the lottery, never have the opportunity to go down to Jerusalem and participate in the temple worship. But Zacharias won the lottery. It was his privilege to be able to preside at the altar of incense and to represent all of the people of Israel before God in prayer. He was not going into the Holy of Holies, and he was not going to offer the sacrificial lamb, but he was going to the altar of incense to pray the pastoral prayer for the nation.

That is why the text says, "The whole multitude of the people was praying outside at the hour of incense." There was a scheduled hour for the assembling together of the saints as a corporate congregation. The priest represented the believers, the congregation, to God. He went to the altar of incense not to pray for himself but to deliver the prayers of the people. While he prayed for the people, they were gathered as a large body, and they also prayed. This was the assembling together of the whole corporation for corporate prayer.

Luke then tells us:

> Then an angel of the Lord appeared to him, standing on the right side of the altar of incense. And

when Zacharias saw him, he was troubled, and fear fell upon him.

But the angel said to him, "Do not be afraid, Zacharias, for your prayer is heard; and your wife Elizabeth will bear you a son." (Luke 1:11–13)

The text makes clear that Zacharias had a major personal problem—he and his wife, Elizabeth, had no children—and that was a great concern to him. However, most commentators agree that the angel Gabriel did not say to Zacharias, "You took this occasion to pray for something for yourself and for your wife—a son." No, Zacharias was a godly and righteous man who would not have violated the sacred office of that moment by praying for himself. His duty was to pray for the nation, for the people. The angel appeared to him and said, "God has heard your prayer for your people. And you're going to have a dramatic part in the answer to this prayer, because you're going to have a son, and your son is going to be the herald of the King, the forerunner of the Messiah."

There is no need to rehearse the remainder of Zacharias's story. What I want us to see is the service he was performing as part of Israel's worship. He was burning incense and praying on behalf of the nation. Prayer was at the center of this act of worship.

However, prayer was not to be the focus only on special occasions in the temple; it was to be a central aspect of the entire temple devotion. Jesus Himself made this clear when He said, "My house shall be called a house of prayer" (Matt. 21:13; Isa. 56:7).

On one occasion, Jesus came to Jerusalem, to the same temple where Zacharias had offered incense on behalf of the people. It was the most sacred site in all of Israel, but Jesus found a very different scene that day. There were sellers of livestock and money changers in the temple area. What were they doing there?

Jewish pilgrims came from all over the world to Jerusalem for the Day of Atonement and for the Passover. As part of those celebrations, they had to make animal sacrifices. They could bring the animals from their homes to the temple, but that was burdensome. To make it easier, herds of animals and large numbers of birds were concentrated in Jerusalem. Jerusalem was like a stockyard. The pilgrims coming to the temple had the opportunity to purchase what they needed to make their sacrifices, and this became a lucrative business. The animals were often sold at an inflated price because of the demand for them. It was similar to ticket scalping at major sporting events in our own time.

The pilgrims to Jerusalem also came with different currencies, and they needed to exchange their home currencies for the one that was used in Israel. If you have ever traveled abroad, you know about exchange rates with the currency, and you also know that not all establishments give the same rate. Some are exploiters and usurious. That was the case with the temple money changers. They afflicted the people with high rates of monetary exchange.

The one time we see Jesus burst into a paroxysm of anger was when He saw this practice going on in the house of God. He fashioned a whip out of cords and overturned the tables of the money changers and the seats of those who sold doves. This was an explosive, incendiary event, just as it would be today. Imagine Jesus coming to a Sunday morning worship service with a whip, and kicking over the pews and knocking down the pulpit. That would be on the front page of the paper the next morning.

Jesus said by way of explanation for His actions, "It is written, 'My house shall be called a house of prayer,' but you have made it a 'den of thieves'" (Matt. 21:13). We could miss the significance of that. Jesus did not call the temple a house of sacrifices or a house of preaching. He called it a house of prayer. The temple's chief designation was that it was to be the focal point of the nation and of the people for prayer.

Do we think of our church buildings today as houses of prayer? When we talk as evangelicals about prayer, we can almost assume that the conversation will be about private and personal prayer, quiet times, daily devotions, or perhaps the Wednesday night prayer meeting where we gather with other Christians to pray. But it is almost completely outside the scope of consideration when we talk about prayer to think about it in terms of the sanctuary. The typical Protestant church building today can hardly be called a house of prayer.

However, when I look at the great leaders of the Reformation, John Calvin and Martin Luther, I see that prayer played a major role in their lives and in the lives of their churches. Seeing that, I cannot help but wonder whether that discipline and their appreciation for prayer in the church were something they brought with them from their Roman Catholic background.

How can we as evangelicals recover the emphasis on prayer in worship that our Reformed forebears understood? Let me mention some ways.

One is to kneel when we pray. Other postures have been used by the people of God at different times and in different places to come before God in prayer. For instance, Calvin speaks of people during the Reformation standing with arms raised to heaven as an attitude of prayer. Kneeling, however, has special significance. In the Old Testament, bowing and kneeling were usually associated with the posture used in the presence of a king. Also, kneeling is a symbolic, dramatic gesture. In the drama, we are communicating something nonverbally even while we are involved in a verbal exercise. It is appropriate, when we come before God to make our requests, to give our intercession, to offer the sacrifice of praise, and to bespeak our thanksgiving, that we kneel.

I hear objections to kneeling, which puzzles me. Perhaps people do not want to be confused with Roman Catholics. They may think, "We do not believe what they believe, so we should not do what they do." That is as foolish as thinking that if a Roman Catholic gives his or her tithe, then that is something we should not do. What could possibly be wrong with assuming a posture of obeisance before God in prayer?

I also hear people say of the church that we have too much time in our liturgy devoted to prayer. I hope they do not say that too loudly. God might hear it. But He already knows if a person is thinking it. We need to be praying more, not less.

In most churches I have attended, prayer is strictly a work of the minister. There is nothing wrong with the minister offering the pastoral prayer; that is exactly what Zacharias did. But I like the fact that while Zacharias was praying, the congregation also entered into prayer. I do not know anything that has transpired in redemptive history that would make that a matter of discontinuity in the New Testament church. It would seem to me that it is pleasing to God when His people participate with the pastor in the corporate prayer.

This involves directed prayer. The pastor directs the congregation to pray by name for those who are ill, then by name for those who are burdened, then those who are at the house of mourning. Individuals in the congregation do not give fifteen-minute orations in prayer, but are able to say aloud the names of the people about whom they are concerned at the moment. It also helps us to know what is on other people's hearts, so that when we are outside of the church we can carry that concern with us.

Prayer is not just a tangential or peripheral part of corporate worship. In ancient Israel, the primary function of worship was the offering of prayer. And so it should be in our churches today. Our sanctuaries should be houses of prayer.

CHAPTER 5
SYMBOLISM IN WORSHIP

Many years ago, when I was a professor at a seminary in Philadelphia, I taught a course on the doctrine of the church and the sacraments. One of my students vigorously opposed any kind of ritual or symbolism, so when I came to the lectures on the Lord's Supper, he expressed his opposition to the sacraments of the church. He grew agitated and said, "Professor Sproul, what difference does it make whether we use bread and wine in the Lord's Supper or Coca-Cola and peanut butter and jelly sandwiches?"

I remember that moment, because something visceral took place within me when he asked that question. However, it was my duty as the professor to stay cool and calm, and not react negatively to the question. So, I looked at the student and (through clenched teeth)

I said, "Because Christ did not consecrate Coca-Cola and peanut butter and jelly sandwiches."

Under extreme circumstances—such as those of people in a concentration camp, who are unable to get the traditional elements to celebrate the Lord's Supper—I do not think God is distressed if other substances are used. But historically, the church has tried to maintain a close connection with that which Christ in fact instituted. The Scriptures tell us that Christ ordained that the Lord's Supper be celebrated with bread and wine, and if we truly want to worship God in the way He directs, we should be willing to use those elements.

In subsequent chapters, we will be examining the sacraments of the New Testament church, baptism and the Lord's Supper. First, however, we need to ask a very fundamental question: Why did God give these rituals to the church, just as He gave similar rites to His Old Testament people?

God's communication to Israel was chiefly verbal, which, we understand, is of central importance in the history of faith and in the life of the church. We have a high view of the importance of God's verbal communication with us. This is why, in Protestantism, we put such an emphasis on the role and place of the Bible. We call the Bible the *verbum Dei*, the "Word of God," or the *vox Dei*, the "voice of God." We consider the verbal communication of God so important to Christianity that throughout history in most Protestant churches the focal point of the sanctuary has been the pulpit, because it is from that position, from that piece of furniture, that the Word of God is proclaimed.

Throughout redemptive history, God always has attended His verbal communication with nonverbal forms of communication: signs, symbols, gestures, drama, concrete object lessons, images, and rituals. These are nonverbal enhancements and reinforcements of the verbal. God not only spoke to His people Israel; He also showed them things.

Consider just a few of the ways God communicated to His people nonverbally. When He made the covenant with Noah, He set the rainbow in the clouds and said, "This is the sign of the covenant which I make between Me and you" (Gen. 9:12a). When He prepared to make His covenant with His people at Sinai, He displayed His majesty to them: "There were thunderings and lightnings, and a thick cloud on the mountain; and the sound of the trumpet was very loud.... Mount Sinai was completely in smoke, because the LORD descended upon it in fire. Its smoke ascended like the smoke of a furnace, and the whole mountain quaked greatly" (Exod. 19:16b–18). Later, when God spoke to the people through His prophets, He often commanded the prophets to communicate His Word through an object lesson. Sometimes these nonverbal lessons were extremely bizarre, such as when God commanded Isaiah to go about naked or when He commanded Hosea to marry a prostitute. Still, these object lessons were a visible way to communicate truth.

Many of the rites God ordained for the Israelite *cultus* were heavily symbolic. We have already considered the symbolic nature of sacrifices and of the incense offerings in the tabernacle and temple. Many of the other rites of the sanctuary were symbolic, as well. Everything from the clothing of the priests to the layout of the tabernacle and the temple had a nonverbal message. There was also the sign of the covenant, circumcision, and the yearly celebration of the Passover. Signs and symbols were common accoutrements of worship in ancient Israel.

It is not hard to understand why God chose to communicate to His people in this way. Such signs and symbols are an inherent part of human communication, and we use them almost intuitively. For instance, when I speak publicly, I use words, but I do not use only words. As I speak, my hands change position. I move around. I furrow my brow. I modulate my voice, raising and lowering it. None of this changes the meaning of the words I use. Rather, these gestures are accoutrements to verbal communication, to reinforce, to enhance, to help deliver the message. Likewise, when we say hello to someone, we reach out to shake the person's hand. What does this gesture mean? It is a sign, a physical signal of peace and of friendship that reinforces the words that we are speaking.

One of the frustrating things for me in my radio teaching is that people can only hear my voice. They cannot see me gesticulating, waving my arms, pacing up and down, and scribbling on the blackboard to reinforce the message. For those of us who grew up in the era before television, our entertainment was through radio, and it was a marvelous exercise of the imagination. I did not only listen to the words that were being spoken in these radio dramas. In my mind's eye, I was seeing the Green Hornet or the Lone Ranger. I had an image in my head of Ma Perkins and young Dr. Malone of the soap operas. There is an advantage, in a real sense, to being restricted simply to hearing the words, because your mind can range freely and conjure up pictures. We dimmed that imaginative power when we became addicted to television. However, TV provides the opportunity for nonverbal communication.

In the same way, when God addresses us, we cannot see His furrowed brow. We cannot see Him gesticulating with His arms. We do not hear the inflections of His voice. The Bible is His written Word, but it is mute. So, God used visual signs as part of His communication with His people. Along with His written Word, He gave a multitude of signs, symbols, external gestures, and rites. The purpose, just as in human communication, was to reinforce that Word.

We have seen that the Old Testament worship of Israel was replete with symbolism, and that was not repudiated or repealed in the New Testament. The New Testament era actually opens with a powerful sign, the appearance of John the Baptist. His message was brief and his words were few, but the whole nation was attracted to hear him because of the "sign" that he was performing by the river Jordan. He told the people that their Messiah was coming, and he then called them to submit to a cleansing rite to prepare them for Christ's advent. Later, of course, Jesus instituted Christian baptism and the Lord's Supper. These two sacraments are the signs and symbols of the New Testament. They are nonverbal dimensions of worship that are exceedingly important to the full expression and full experience of our meeting with God in worship.

When I refer to the sacraments as signs and symbols, I am not being redundant. We tend to use the words *sign* and *symbol* as synonyms, but there is a subtle distinction. A sign points beyond itself to another reality. The Greek word *semeion* is used frequently in the New Testament, particularly in John's gospel with respect to the ministry of Christ. Jesus did not just preach and teach, but He gave signs. The gospel writers might say, "This sign [*semeion*] Jesus did at Capernaum" or "This sign Jesus did at Cana." These signs He did, such as turning the water into wine at Cana, were not verbal. They were nonverbal. Jesus did something in the outward, visible world that was "significant," that pointed beyond itself to a deeper truth.

A symbol, however, goes deeper. Paul Tillich, the twentieth-century theologian, got at the distinction through an illustration similar to the one that follows: you're heading to Daytona Beach, and you see a sign that says, "Daytona Beach, 14 miles." The function of that sign is to point you on the way, to point you toward a reality that is beyond itself. But when you drive your car that fourteen miles, you see another sign, one that says, "Entering Daytona Beach." The sign that says, "Entering Daytona Beach," is not Daytona Beach. But it differs from the first sign in this subtle way: it is not Daytona Beach, but it participates in Daytona Beach. This illustrates the subtle distinction Tillich was getting at between the sign and the symbol. The symbol not only points beyond itself, but is itself part of the reality, so that the symbol escalates the intensity of the sign to another level.

John Calvin was engaged constantly in debates about liturgy and the sacraments, particularly about the Lord's Supper, because he was concerned that the elements of the Lord's Supper be regarded as symbols, not as *nuda signa*, as naked or empty signs. He sought to show not only that the signs point beyond themselves, but also that they are part of the reality that we engage in at the Lord's Table.

Students have asked me, "Did John Calvin believe in the real presence of Christ at the Lord's Supper?" I respond, "Absolutely," and they look at me stunned. They say, "You cannot be serious. I did not think Presbyterians believed in the real presence of Christ at the Lord's Supper." I tell them to read the Presbyterian creeds and to look at the confessions. It is a central point of our doctrine that we believe that Christ is really present at Holy Communion.

Calvin's stance focused on the word *substance*. When Calvin debated the Lutherans over the manner of Christ's presence in the Lord's Supper, he emphatically denied that Christ was substantially present in the sacrament. Yet when he debated with the Zwinglians, he insisted upon using the word *substance* with respect to the presence of Jesus at the Supper. Was Calvin blatantly contradicting himself? Not at all, because the term *substance* can refer to physical substance or it can signify that which is real.

On one side of the controversy, the word *substance* focused on the question of whether Christ's corporeal or physical body was in any way present immediately at the Lord's Supper. Calvin said that Christ's body is in heaven. It is not on the Communion table. His body has ascended, and He is at the right hand of God the Father. People then assumed that Calvin thought Christ was really not at the Lord's Supper. Calvin would assure them that He is there, and He is there spiritually. So, people responded: "Oh, you mean He is there in our minds; He is there as a memorial, symbolically?" Calvin would reply: "No. He is there really. He is there touching His divine nature and His divine substance, which is real, not imaginary. If by spiritual, you mean fictional, that is not correct. The real spiritual presence of Jesus Christ is at the Lord's Table."

The point of this is not to get into a discussion about the various views of the presence of Christ or the meaning of the sacrament of the Lord's Supper, but simply to show how crucial the nonverbal or symbolic elements of worship were in the minds of the Reformers. Both Calvin and Luther were keenly concerned to maintain, along with the preaching of the Word of God, the function of the nonverbal signs of the Word of God, which God Himself instituted.

Like the Reformers, we must never underestimate the importance of the verbal element of worship, the preaching of the Word of God. But we must not forget that God, when He outlined His pattern for worship in the Old Testament, also mandated visible signs, tangible acts of drama that are not isolated from the Word or contrary to the Word but are married to the Word. That is why, for example, in most Christian churches, you are not allowed to celebrate the sacrament without some preaching to indicate that Word and sacrament go together. The Word is expressed verbally, and then that verbal expression is supported, corroborated, and reinforced by the drama of the signs and of the symbols.

CHAPTER 6
BAPTISM, PART 1

I can usually stump my seminary students by asking them this question: Who was the greatest prophet in the Old Testament? When I ask that question, the students often get into an argument. Some say Elijah; others say Isaiah; still others name Jeremiah, Ezekiel, or Daniel; and the debate goes on. Finally I say, "No, the greatest prophet in the Old Testament was John the Baptist."

How do you suppose they respond to that answer? They say: "That is not fair. He is in the New Testament." Yes, John's story comes to us in the section of the Bible that is called the New Testament, but the historical period in which he operated was that of the old covenant. The new covenant began in the upper room, when Jesus celebrated the Passover with His friends. It was there that He reinterpreted the significance of the Seder meal and ratified the new covenant He would make with His people in His own blood on the following day. Jesus said, "The law and the prophets were until John" (Luke 16:16a). The Greek word that is translated "until" means "up to and including." So, in terms of redemptive history, the old covenant was still in effect when John ministered. That is important to our understanding of the significance of his ministry of baptism, and of Jesus's submission to baptism at John's hands.

John is not called "the Baptist" because of his denominational affiliation but because of the function he performed. Literally, he was "John the baptizer." It is interesting that he is called John the Baptist, since he performed more than one function. His giving of baptism was only supplemental to the primary function he was called to perform in redemptive history, which was to be the forerunner of the Messiah, the herald of the King. John is known in the New Testament itself, as well as in church history, as "the Baptist," because in performing his primary function, he introduced baptism to Israel in such an extraordinary way that he became identified with that function rather than his role as Christ's forerunner.

I find that there is vast confusion about the baptism of John and the baptism of Jesus. Many, if not most, Christians make the assumption that the baptism Christ instituted in the New Testament (the baptism we perform in the church today) is simply a direct continuation of the rite initiated by John. However, the baptism of the New Testament is not identical with John's baptism. There is significant continuity between the two baptisms, but there is also a significant element of discontinuity.

To help alleviate this confusion, let us trace the development of the baptistic rite historically. In the Old Testament, there was no specific provision for baptism, but a precursor of baptism was established very early in Jewish history. Then there was a major innovation or variation of baptism later in Jewish history. An even more dramatic change came with the ministry of John the Baptist.

The seeds for the concept of baptism are found in the Old Testament story of Noah. The waters of the flood were the element God used to destroy the world, but the waters also were that which floated the ark and made it possible for Noah and his family to survive. They were saved from the waters by the waters, as Peter wrote, "Eight souls, were saved through water" (1 Pet. 3:20b). The same dual usage is seen in the Israelites' crossing of the Red Sea. The waters that parted for the Israelites to cross through returned to their place and destroyed the Egyptians. Paul wrote that the people of Israel were "baptized into Moses" (1 Cor. 10:2a), showing that the Red Sea deliverance was a kind of forecast or precursor of the New Testament baptism of the people of God into Jesus Christ.

Water played a significant role in the Israelite liturgy, where one of the articles in the tabernacle and in the temple was the laver. The priests had to wash themselves in the laver as part of a purification rite. This rite had symbolic significance—it showed that the priests were dirty. The idea was that, as sinners, people come into the presence of God as polluted creatures. The priests needed to undergo a liturgical rite at the laver of washing that symbolized the people's need to be cleansed from sin.

When I was in seminary, my mentor, Dr. John Gerstner, generally would preach in one of the little country churches in and around Pittsburgh each Sunday morning. One day the elders met with him before the service and asked if Dr. Gerstner would lead the church through the service of infant baptism. They explained that they had a particular tradition in their infant baptism service that they wanted him to follow.

"As the parents present their child for baptism, we give them a white rose, which is attached to the baptismal gown or clothing of the infant that is being brought for baptism," the men said.

Dr. Gerstner asked what the white rose was to represent, and they answered that it represented innocence.

"Oh, I see," he said. "So, you want me to give them a white rose to symbolize the child's innocence, and then you want me to baptize the child with water?"

"Yes."

"What does the water symbolize?" Dr. Gerstner queried.

"Cleansing," they said.

"Cleansing from what?"

"Well, from sin."

Dr. Gerstner said, "There is something here I do not understand." They got the point, and that was the end of the white rose tradition at that church. If babies are innocent, they do not need to be baptized.

God instituted the washing ritual at the laver in the tabernacle to signify that every human being needed to be washed because every human being had been tainted by sin. Every baby is born into this world in sin. Though not yet guilty of any actual sin, each infant carries the weight of the fallen human nature, bearing original sin. Original sin is not the first sin of Adam and Eve but the result of the first sin, that is, the fall of the human race into corruption. As David cried in the Old Testament, "Behold, I was brought forth in iniquity, and in sin my mother conceived me" (Ps. 51:5).

As Israel's history progressed, a ritual called proselyte baptism developed. A proselyte is a convert from one religion to another. We do not find a strong emphasis on evangelism in the community life of the Jewish people in the Old Testament. In fact, modern Judaism finds the evangelism of the Christian agenda reprehensible. Jews are often outspoken on this point. They think that Christians should keep to themselves and not talk to Jews about Christianity, because, after all, Jews do not try to proselytize other people.

I have asked my Jewish friends if they believe that Judaism is the truth, and they respond that they do. I then ask, "Do you believe that my conviction that Christ is the Son of God is the truth?" and they say no. Next I question, "So, you think I have erred from the truth by embracing this distortion that you say undermines monotheism and the purity of the faith once delivered to Moses?" They say yes to that. So, I conclude by asking: "If you believe that I am missing the truth, why do not you care enough about me to try to lead me out of my error and into the household of faith? If you care about me, if you really think that what you believe is the truth, why won't you tell me about it?" At that, they usually scratch their heads and say nothing. Jews have an antipathy toward evangelism that is very deeply rooted in their history.

That is why, in the Old Testament, we do not see much evangelism. Yet, the mandate was there. When God made His covenant with Abraham, He called Abraham and the people of God to be a light to the nations. We see the story of Jonah, who was called to be a missionary, involved in proselytizing. He reached out to the pagans and led them into the household of faith. So, while we do not see a great emphasis on evangelism and missionary outreach in the Old Testament, it did occur.

God chose the Jews from all the nations of the world to be a holy nation, His covenant people. There was a sharp distinction between the Jews and the other ethnic groups, known as "the Gentiles." A Gentile is a non-Jew, someone who is a part of one of the many other ethnic groups or nations. The Jews considered the Gentiles to be strangers, foreigners, and aliens to the covenant, and so they were. They were outside the covenant community, outside the household of Israel. Because they were strangers, foreigners, and aliens to the household of faith, they were considered unclean. Rather than pitying the Gentiles and reaching out to them, the Jews gradually developed a pride in their status as God's chosen people and came to spurn the Gentiles.

There were certain processes the Jews had to go through to become true members of the household of faith. A male had to be circumcised as a baby and then, at age thirteen, he had to undergo a rite similar to Christian confirmation, the *bar mitzvah*. The Hebrew word *bar* means "son of." For instance, the name Simon Bar-Jonah meant "Simon, son of Jonah." The word *mitzvah* is based on the Hebrew word that meant "commandment," so a Jewish male at age thirteen became a "son of the commandment." Having studied the teachings of the Torah, he embraced them for his own and professed his faith in the teaching of the Law and of the Prophets. He then became a full-fledged member of the covenant community. So, two things were required of Jewish males, circumcision and a profession of faith. Likewise, Jewish women went through their own confirmation rites. Then they were full members in the covenant community.

What about a Gentile who wanted to convert to Judaism? It was possible for a Gentile to enter into Judaism, but a male had to do three things. He had to be circumcised and make a profession of faith (that is, receive the teachings of Moses), both of which the Jewish male had to do. In addition, the Gentile male had to undergo the ritual called proselyte baptism. He had to go through a cleansing rite, because as a Gentile he was considered unclean.

In the New Testament, particularly the book of Acts, we find that the early church had to deal with different groups of people in its outreach. There were Jews, Samaritans, and Gentiles. There was also a group called the God-fearers. Cornelius, the Roman centurion to whom Peter preaches in Acts 10, is designated as a God-fearer. A God-fearer was a Gentile who had converted to Judaism and who had met all of the requirements except for circumcision. It is easy to imagine that an adult male Gentile, desiring to come into Judaism, would say, "I love Judaism, so I'll embrace the faith and I'll take the bath, but I'll pass on circumcision." They did not have anesthetics to make surgery more bearable as we have today, so such people were considered God-fearing Gentiles. That meant they were believers in Judaism, but they had not met all the requirements for full membership in the covenant community.

That is why it is significant that Pentecost is repeated in Acts. On the day of Pentecost, the Holy Spirit was poured out on people from every nation, but they were all Jews from different cities (Acts 2). They all had come to Jerusalem for the Jewish festival. Later, the Spirit fell on Samaritan believers (Acts 8), on the God-fearers in Cornelius's household (Acts 10), and finally, at Ephesus, on Gentiles (Acts 19). So, all four of these groups were given this outpouring of the Holy Spirit in the book of Acts.

In ancient Israel, the baptismal rite was restricted to Gentiles. When Malachi died, the voice of prophecy ceased in Israel, and for four hundred years God was silent. The prophetic office was interrupted. There was a moratorium on special revelation through the mouths of prophets. But the last prophecy of the Old Testament predicted that, before the coming of the Messiah, Elijah would return (Mal. 4:5), and so the Jewish people continued to watch for the reappearance of Elijah.

Today, when the Jews celebrate the Passover, there is always an empty chair at the head of the table. That chair is in place in the event Elijah should come. The Jews are still waiting for the Messiah, and one of the reasons they are waiting for Him is that they believe Elijah has not come. Since Malachi said that Elijah must come, the fact that he apparently has not means the Messiah has not come either.

After four hundred years of prophetic silence, out of the desert came a man who dressed and acted like Elijah, and who came as a prophet. The New Testament sees John not just as one of many prophets but as the prophet par excellence, because he did not just prophesy the future coming of the Messiah. His role, as the angel explained to Zacharias, was to be the forerunner or the herald of the Messiah. John was to introduce the Messiah and announce the presence of the King. He came in order to announce the advent of the Christ.

John's basic message was repentance. The first thing he said was, "Repent, for the kingdom of God is at hand!" (Matt. 3:2). In other words, he called the people to repent not because the kingdom of God would come someday in the distant future but because it was coming very soon. The force of his language was that the kingdom was about to break through. He used two very meaningful images to support that statement. He said the ax was laid at the root of the tree, and the winnowing fork was in the Messiah's hand (Matt.

3:10–12). These images conveyed the idea that the moment of crisis, of supreme judgment for the earth, was at hand because the Messiah was about to appear on the stage of history. John basically said to the Jews, "You're not ready," and he called them to repent.

Not only did he call them to repent, but he called them to be baptized. This was so radical a call that John was probably in jeopardy of being executed for heresy and for blasphemy. He called Jewish people to submit to a ritual that heretofore had been reserved exclusively for pagans and for Gentiles. The force of his message was this: "In God's sight right now, you people are so sinful and polluted that you are, as it were, just like the Gentiles. So, repent and be baptized." It was as if God was saying through John, "My own people are unclean, and My own people need to take a bath."

In response to John's call, thousands of common people flocked to him. They were excited by his message that the Messiah was coming. They realized they were sinners and knew they were not ready for the Messiah. So, they willingly submitted to baptism at the hands of John. Only the Pharisees and the Sadducees, the clergy, the officials at Jerusalem, demurred. They said: "This madman is telling these people that they have to act like the Gentiles. But we do not need cleansing. We are the children of Abraham." In response John said: "Brood of vipers! … God is able to raise up children to Abraham from these stones" (Matt. 3:7b–9). There was tremendous conflict between John and the religious authorities.

In the midst of all of this, Jesus appeared. When He came, John sang the *Agnus Dei*, declaring: "Behold! The Lamb of God who takes away the sin of the world!" (John 1:29b). Then, to John's utter amazement, Jesus asked John to baptize Him. John tried to prevent it. He said, "I need to be baptized by You, and are You coming to me?" (Matt. 3:14b). It was as if John were saying, "God forbid! I cannot baptize You; You're the Lamb without blemish. You're sinless; You're the Messiah. This would be a travesty of theology if I were to baptize You. Jesus, You should baptize me." Jesus replied, "Permit it to be so now, for thus it is fitting for us to fulfill all righteousness" (Matt. 3:15b). John was persuaded, so they went down into the Jordan, and Jesus was baptized by John.

What did Jesus mean when He said, "Permit it to be so now, for thus it is fitting for us to fulfill all righteousness"? What did the Messiah need to do in order to be the Lamb of God, in order to make an atonement for the people of Israel? We know that Jesus came to die for our sins, but why did He not simply come down from heaven on Good Friday, go to the cross, arise on Easter, and go back to heaven? It was because Christ's work on the cross was only half of His mission. In order for Jesus to die for our sins, it was first necessary for Him to fulfill the role that Adam failed to fulfill. He had to fulfill all righteousness. Jesus had to pass the test in the wilderness. He had to resist temptation. And He had to obey the law of God. In other words, we are saved by two things: the death of Christ and the life of Christ. The death of Christ covers our sin, but the life of Christ provides the merit and the righteousness that we must have in order to enter into heaven. So, Jesus's life is as important for us as His death. He lived to fulfill all of the law of God.

Now, God had added a new law through John the Baptist. We must remember, John was a prophet of God. He was acting as Elijah, although there was confusion about that. The Pharisees asked John, "Who are you? ... Are you Elijah?" and John replied, "I am not" (John 1:19b–21b), but Jesus said, "I say to you that Elijah has come already," and His disciples "understood that He spoke to them of John the Baptist" (Matt. 17:12–13). Jesus was not saying that John the Baptist was the reincarnation of Elijah. He affirmed what the angel said to John's father, Zacharias: "He will go before [the Messiah] in the spirit and power of Elijah" (Luke 1:17a ESV). John's ministry was the revisiting, the renewing, of the office of Elijah. So, John, speaking as a prophet on the order of Elijah, commanded that all God's people be baptized in preparation for a new covenant.

Thus, when Jesus came to John to be baptized, He said, in effect: "I have to fulfill all the requirements, not because I am a sinner, but because I must represent the nation. Since the nation is required to be circumcised, I am required to be circumcised, and since the nation is required now to be baptized, I must submit to baptism." Jesus submitted to baptism out of obedience to His Father.

There is continuity between the baptism that John administered and the baptism that we experience. Both baptisms signify a cleansing from sin, and both signify an involvement in the kingdom of God, among other things, but the meaning of New Testament baptism takes on a much more expansive content than the limited significance that we find in John's baptism. The two baptisms are not the same thing. The baptism that is given in the Trinitarian formula and that is commanded in the New Testament to the church has a much deeper and broader content, meaning, and significance, and we will turn our attention to that subject in the next chapter.

CHAPTER 7

BAPTISM, PART 2

It has been my experience that the average person in the church today has little understanding of the significance of New Testament baptism. In fact, as someone who has participated in a multitude of ordination exams, I can say that very few ministers have an understanding of the expansive significance of baptism as we understand it Apostolically and historically. I think everyone knows that baptism is a sign of cleansing, but it is much more than that. It has references to many dimensions of the Christian life.

It is important that we understand these references, for several reasons. First, as we have seen, God uses nonverbal signs and symbols to reinforce and emphasize the verbal promises that He makes. Second, New Testament baptism is not simply a sign; it is *the* sign. In the old covenant, the covenant God made with Abraham, the sign was circumcision. The sign of the new covenant is baptism. Third, it is easy, as we have seen, going back to the distinction between Cain and Abel, for a person to observe the outward sign and miss the significance, either because the significance is not understood by the mind or, as in the case of Cain, is not understood in the heart. The result is that the sign becomes almost naked or empty. If we are to continue these signs in the life of the church, it is imperative that we understand what they mean. Even that is not enough. We have to embrace the significance behind these signs with our hearts if we are going to please God. Fourth, we are called, as Jesus's disciples, to give the sign of baptism to every Christian. Because of that, it is important that we have an understanding of what it is and what it does.

When we speak of New Testament baptism, we are speaking of that sign Jesus instituted when He commanded His disciples, saying, "Go therefore and make disciples of all the nations, baptizing them in the name of the Father and of the Son and of the Holy Spirit" (Matt. 28:19). As we saw, this was different from the baptism that was practiced by John the Baptist. John's baptism was not a covenantal sign. His baptism was simply a sign of repentance given to Jews in preparation for the coming of the Messiah.

So, the question before us is this: What does New Testament baptism, the baptism that was instituted by Jesus, signify? There are several possible answers.

First, baptism is the sign of the new covenant. A covenant is an agreement that involves promises and obligations. In the Bible, a covenant is a promise of God, and the new covenant is God's promise of salvation through faith in the person and work of Jesus Christ. On the night of His betrayal, as Jesus celebrated the

Passover meal with His disciples, He took the cup and said, "For this is My blood of the new covenant, which is shed for many for the remission of sins" (Matt. 26:28). By shedding His blood, by giving His life, Jesus made atonement for the sins of His people, and the promise of the new covenant is that if we put our trust in Christ, in His righteousness, and in His atonement, God will give us salvation, eternal life with Him. Baptism is the sign of that covenant. In the broadest sense, baptism signifies everything God promises His people in the new covenant. It is a sign of every benefit He bestows upon us.

The sign of the old covenant, the covenant God made with Abraham and with Israel, was circumcision. What did circumcision signify? Old Testament scholars tell us it had a positive signification and a negative signification. The positive signification was that God consecrated the person receiving it and the Jewish nation. He set them apart. They were marked as being cut apart from the rest of the world, a people with whom God had entered into a special covenantal and redemptive relationship. The negative signification was that the person said, in essence: "God, if I fail to keep the terms of the covenant, may I be cut off from all of Your benefits. May I be cut off from Your presence even as I have cut off the foreskin of my flesh." So, circumcision was both a positive and a negative sign.

Many New Testament scholars believe that dual aspect carries over into the new covenant. They believe that just as baptism is a sign of all the blessings that are promised to those who receive Christ, it is also a sign of the curse that will fall upon us if we repudiate the terms of the new covenant. We will drown in our sins and will be inundated by the flood of God's wrath for our apostasy.

Second, baptism is a sign of rebirth. In John 3, Jesus engaged in a conversation with a Pharisee named Nicodemus, who came to Him by night. Jesus told him: "Unless one is born again, he cannot see the kingdom of God.... Unless one is born of water and the Spirit, he cannot enter the kingdom of God. That which is born of the flesh is flesh, and that which is born of the Spirit is spirit" (John 3:3–6).

This is a very difficult passage, and theologians and exegetes have been divided for centuries about the precise meaning of Jesus's words. Clearly, however, He was speaking about the spiritual transformation that theologians call regeneration. What is regeneration? The root of the word *regeneration* is the Greek *genao*, which means "to be, become, or happen." The same root is found in the word *genesis*, as in the book of Genesis, which has to do with the beginning. We note that the word *regeneration* begins with the prefix *re*, which means "again." When we redo something, repaint something, or rework something, we do that task again. So, we have a regenesis—a new generation, a new birth; it is like starting over.

That is what regeneration means, but what is the content of this word doctrinally? What has the church understood that takes place when a human being undergoes regeneration? Clearly it is a spiritual genesis, because Jesus makes a distinction between the flesh and the spirit. When Jesus spoke of "flesh," He was not thinking of just the body. We know this because He did not use the Greek word *soma*, which can refer specifically to the physical body of a person. Instead, He used the word *sarx*, which also can refer to the physical body but specifically has reference in the Bible to our sinful nature: that fallen, corrupt state into which we are born. Jesus said this "flesh," this fallen nature, profits nothing—and Martin Luther noted that

that nothing is not a little something. The Bible tells us that when we come into this world as fallen creatures, creatures of the flesh, we are biologically alive. We have what the Greek language calls *bios*, which means "life." But we are in a state called "flesh," a sinful state that profits nothing. In other words, we are in a state of spiritual death. We need to be raised to new life in order to respond to God.

In spiritual terms, the Bible says that fallen people are at enmity with God. The only feeling of their disposition with respect to God is a disinclination toward God. The pagans, the unbelievers, are never in a neutral state with respect to God. In their hearts, they are anti-God. They are fugitives from God. They reject God. They refuse to have God in their thinking, and their natural disposition is opposition toward the living God. Clearly then, such people need a spiritual regeneration, a fundamental change in their hearts.

The way in which regeneration is understood differs from church to church in subtle, sometimes insignificant, ways. But apart from dispensationalism, which was a nineteenth-century departure from orthodoxy, the rest of the Christian world agrees at least on this: the essential point of regeneration is that God works internally on the soul of a person and changes the disposition of his or her heart. In other words, regeneration has always been seen as the antidote to original sin. The doctrine of original sin describes the degree of the fallen, corrupt nature that we inherit from Adam. Unfortunately, the Roman Catholic Church has one view of original sin, the Lutherans have another view, the Methodists another, the Presbyterians another, and so on. These denominations do not agree on the details of original sin, and that is primarily why they do not all agree on the details of regeneration. But each one agrees that humanity is seriously, radically fallen by nature, and that regeneration deals with this inherent and inherited corruption.

No matter how we understand regeneration, baptism is a sign of it. Baptism symbolizes the new birth. It is a sign of spiritual resurrection, of spiritual renewal, of being brought from spiritual death to spiritual life, and the church has understood this signification from its earliest days.

Third, baptism is a sign of our identification with Christ. Two aspects of Christ are signified by baptism: His humiliation and His exaltation. Let's look at these in reverse order.

The Apostle Paul described Jesus as "the firstborn from the dead" (Col. 1:18), and he wrote to the Romans, "For whom [the Father] foreknew, He also predestined to be conformed to the image of His Son, that He might be the firstborn among many brethren" (8:29). Paul was saying that while Christ was the first to be exalted by being raised bodily from the dead, He will not be the last, for all of those who are His will be raised from death, too. Christ was raised from death as the firstborn of many brothers. He is "the firstfruits of those who have fallen asleep" (1 Cor. 15:20). We who belong to Him will be raised to eternal life someday.

But the blessings do not end there. Christ has been appointed as "heir of all things" (Heb. 1:2), and Paul described us as "heirs of God and joint heirs with Christ" (Rom. 8:17). When Christ was raised from the dead, He inherited the kingship. Jesus said there will come a day when He will say to the righteous, "Come, you blessed of My Father, inherit the kingdom prepared for you from the foundation of the world" (Matt. 25:34). We will inherit a kingdom because we are in Christ. All that is His is ours.

I once heard my mentor, Dr. John Gerstner, explain justification and the imputation of Christ's righteousness. He said, "In justification, when you put your faith in Christ, truly trust Him for your salvation, in the sight of God all that Christ has and all that Christ is becomes yours." In this identification, in our salvation, all that Christ is and all that Christ has becomes ours in the sight of God. When I heard this, I realized that when God looks at me, He sees the merit of Christ. My salvation rests not on my performance, but on His. That is why I labored the point in the previous chapter that we are redeemed not only by the death of Christ but also by the life of Christ. He fulfilled every jot and tittle of the law and won the blessing that was promised to the people of the old covenant, to anyone who keeps the law. Jesus kept the law for you and for me and received the reward for us.

We have these marvelous promises that we will participate in the glory that the Father has bestowed upon Christ. We are going to go to heaven. We are going to be kings and priests. We are going to inherit the kingdom that the Father has prepared for His beloved Son. God is going to include us in His exaltation of His Son. Those are the wonderful promises Paul conveyed to us. But every time he did, he warned us that unless we are prepared and willing to participate in the humiliation and the afflictions of Christ, His inheritance will not belong to us.

I hear complaints from people in the church who ask, "How can God allow Christians to suffer the way they do?" I hear preachers say, "We are not supposed to suffer as Christians." When I hear that, I want to say, "You are a false prophet." Not only are we allowed to suffer, but it is our vocation as Christians. Our Savior was a suffering

Savior, a Man of sorrows and acquainted with grief, who endured manifold afflictions. The New Testament tells us many times to be prepared for the same thing. We suffer, if need be, for a season. Peter said, "Beloved, do not think it strange concerning the fiery trial which is to try you, as though some strange thing happened to you" (1 Pet. 4:12). The thing that is strange is when we enjoy relative freedom from afflictions in this world. The time when afflictions are over will come when we pass through the veil.

If any of those reading this book attend my funeral, I hope they will not grieve for me. You can grieve for me the week before I die, if I am scared and hurting, but when I gasp that last fleeting breath and my immortal soul flees to heaven, I am going to be jumping over fire hydrants down the golden streets, and my biggest concern, if I have any, will be my wife back here grieving. When I die, I will be identified with Christ's exaltation. But right now, I am identified with His affliction.

Of course, none of us likes to suffer, for any reason. However, if someone slanders me because of my stance for the gospel or hurts me because I am a Christian, that is one kind of pain or suffering. But to wake up in the middle of the night with a bleeding ulcer is a different kind of suffering. When we are suffering in our warfare with pagan forces that are against us, it is somewhat easier to bear because we know we are bearing it for the gospel's sake. But when we awaken with excruciating pain and are rushed to the emergency room, how does that relate to the kingdom of God?

Let's look at it this way. What is the difference whether I am assaulted by human beings' animosity to the things of God or whether I am afflicted by the forces of sin and darkness through bodily disease? Disease is part of the fallen world. It is part of the kingdom of this world. To bear that affliction is to give the same testimony to the redemption that is ours in Christ as if we were bearing the affliction of the persecutions of the emperor Nero. Our spiritual response to disease should be no different from our spiritual response to persecution.

In Colossians, Paul made a mysterious statement: "I ... fill up in my flesh what is lacking in the afflictions of Christ, for the sake of His body, which is the church" (Col. 1:24). Appealing to that passage, the Roman Catholic Church developed a merit system for saints who perform works of supererogation, people such as martyrs. The Roman Church said there is a treasury of merit that includes the merit of Christ plus the merit of the saints, and the church can borrow from that treasury for people who are deficient in merit in order to decrease their time in purgatory. Historically, Rome has appealed to this passage in Colossians to support this idea.

The Reformers of the sixteenth century found that idea repugnant. The Reformation statement was that Christ paid it all, that His suffering and affliction were all-sufficient. The Reformers declared emphatically that there is nothing lacking in the merit of Christ's suffering.

What did Paul mean when he talked about filling up that which is lacking in the afflictions of Christ if there is no deficiency of merit in Christ's suffering? Christ, who performed the perfect sacrifice once and for all, nevertheless called His church to bear witness to His suffering until He returns, and there is still a measure of suffering that must take place in the history of redemption. This suffering will not add anything to Christ's merit. Our suffering does not atone for anyone's sin, certainly not for our own, but God's redemptive historical plan has to be finished, and that plan includes the afflictions of the people of God. Paul, being acutely conscious of that, spoke of his filling up the agenda of suffering, and you and I must do the same.

There is an authentic identification of God's people with Christ's humiliation and His exaltation, and that identification with Christ is signified by baptism. An individual's baptism says to the world, "I belong to Christ and He belongs to me." For this reason, the New Testament speaks of our being buried with Christ in baptism. Our baptism signifies our identity with Him in His humiliation and in His exaltation—in His suffering and in His resurrection.

Our Baptist friends are frequently critical of churches that practice infant baptism or those that baptize by sprinkling or dipping. They believe that the outward sign loses something when the church moves away from immersion because the immersion process more graphically communicates the sign of burial, going under the water, and resurrection, coming up out of the water. From an experiential viewpoint, I think they are right. It is more dramatic to go under and come up. Virtually all the churches that practice dipping and sprinkling took the position historically that the preferential mode of baptism was immersion. Even Calvin said that it was better to immerse than to sprinkle. I would say that as well today, though immersion is not required for baptism to be authentic.

Fourth, baptism is a sign of cleansing from sin. Baptism is a sign of forgiveness. It is a sign of justification. It is a sign of total cleansing, of sanctification, of glorification. In other words, everything that is involved in the process and the complete work of salvation is indicated by baptism. It is a sign of salvation.

These, then, are some of the major truths that are signified by baptism. We could add that baptism is a sign of faith. Historically, nearly every church has held that baptism signifies faith, which is why many churches will not give the sign if faith, or at least a profession of faith, is not present. Also, baptism is deemed to be a sign of repentance. Finally, it is also thought to be a sign of the baptism of the Holy Spirit.

I noted above that it is crucial for us to understand the meaning behind the sign of baptism because it is all too common for us human beings to observe the sign and miss the significance. As I close this chapter, I want to return to that point. Hear these words of Paul from Romans 2:25–29:

> For circumcision is indeed profitable if you keep the law; but if you are a breaker of the law, your circumcision has become uncircumcision. Therefore, if an uncircumcised man keeps the righteous requirements of the law, will not his uncircumcision be counted as circumcision? And will not the physically uncircumcised, if he fulfills the law, judge you who, even with your written code and circumcision, are a transgressor of the law? For he is not a Jew who is one outwardly, nor is circumcision that which is outward in the flesh; but he is a Jew who is one inwardly; and circumcision is that of the

> heart, in the Spirit, not in the letter; whose praise is not from men, but from God.

This passage does not say anything about baptism specifically, but what Paul said here flew right in the face of many of the rabbis of his day. Paul instructed that the outward sign of circumcision in Israel did not automatically guarantee the inward reality. In fact, Paul said it is possible to have the inward reality without the outward sign.

Unfortunately, there are denominations that believe that the very giving of baptism is rebirth, that it automatically cleanses away sin. It would be nice to get rid of original sin and to get regeneration in that way. I would spend the rest of my life with a fire hose if salvation worked like that. I would baptize everybody in my sight if it automatically communicated redemption, but it does not work that way.

The response of many Protestants is to ask, "Well, if baptism does not automatically convey the grace of regeneration, why do it?" The reason is the promise of God. His promise of all these blessings, for all who believe, is signified by the sign our Lord instituted and commanded to be taken to all nations.

I know that baptism does not save me, but I also know that I am saved. When Satan comes to assault me, I can look at the Devil and say, "I am baptized. I bear the sign of the promise of God." When I say that, I am saying: "I trust in this promise, Satan, for it is God's promise. Since it is God's promise, though my faith is fallible and fragile, the promise of God cannot be broken, and I hold on to the pledge of that promise that is mine in baptism." I am afraid that is the point the church has not gotten.

Sometimes a person will say to me that because he was baptized as an infant and did not understand the significance of baptism when the sign was put upon him, now, having come to faith and to an understanding of what God has done for him, he wants to be baptized once more. I have to tell him no. Why do I say that? When we are baptized the first time, we receive an outward sign of the promise of God, and when we come to faith, God has kept His promise. We are now born-again. We are now members of the new covenant. We now enjoy in the sight of God personal identification with Jesus Christ. We now participate in His humiliation and the exaltation. What part of the promise has God failed to keep? None. God in time and space has fulfilled every aspect of that promise. So, I will not let a person say to God, "Run that by me again—I am not sure You meant it."

I realize no one intends that when he or she asks to be rebaptized. They are looking for a spiritual experience, but I want them to understand why I cannot do it. I want them to understand how blessed they are that that sign they had outwardly has now been realized inwardly, so that now they are living proof of the trustworthiness of the promises of God.

CHAPTER 8
TO YOU AND YOUR CHILDREN

There are few, if any, issues in the life of the church about which Christians are more divided than the question of whether infants should be baptized. There is a host of churches that practice infant baptism, and there are many others that practice what is called "believers' baptism," restricting the sacrament to those who are old enough to make a profession of faith prior to receiving baptism. Between these groups, there is much agreement about the nature of baptism, although there are also some elements of disagreement that go across denominational lines. But the major issue of contention concerns who is to receive this sacrament.

It is important to remember that both positions are motivated by a desire to do what is biblical and what is pleasing to God. Churches that practice infant baptism believe that it is their duty to baptize infants, and in failing to do so they would be derelict in a responsibility. Those that refrain from infant baptism do so out of a concern and motivation not to insert something into the life of the church that is not sanctioned by Scripture. So, both sides are motivated by a desire to do what is pleasing to God, and we should grant that up front.

There is nothing in the New Testament that explicitly teaches or commands the practice of infant baptism. The New Testament nowhere says, "Thou shalt baptize infants." Neither is there an explicit example of infant baptism in the New Testament, a narrative that gives a clear indication that an infant was baptized in the early church. The other side of the coin is that there is nothing in the New Testament that explicitly forbids the baptism of infants or explicitly teaches that a profession of faith is a necessary prerequisite for receiving the sacrament. There are passages that may seem to teach these things by way of inference and implication, but both sides agree that these teachings are not explicit. Therefore, in any discussions about this highly controversial issue, there should be an extra measure of forbearance among the brothers and the sisters of the Lord, recognizing that we are dealing with a debate that rests ultimately on inferences and implications drawn from Scripture, not on explicit teachings. Since we have no explicit command or prohibition, we have to be a little gentler with each other.

That is not to say that both sides on this issue are correct. That clearly cannot be the case. Unless you are a blatant relativist, you understand that the practice of infant baptism is either something God wants us to do or something He does not want us to do. God may be pleased with both sides' motives, but that does not mean that

He is pleased with the actual positions of both sides. So, it is important for us to grapple with this issue and come to an understanding and a conviction as to what the Bible teaches.

As a seminary professor, I encourage my students to wrestle with this issue. I usually have a mixed group—Baptists, Presbyterians, Episcopalians, and others. When we deal with the question of baptism, I sometimes have those who come from the tradition that practices infant baptism write a paper on the case for believers' baptism, and I assign my Baptist students a paper on the case for infant baptism. I do this not to force students from either side to be persuaded of the other position. I simply want them to walk away from the class not necessarily agreeing with the other position but at least understanding it, having been forced to grapple with it.

I will put my cards on the table up front and say that as one who is a Presbyterian in his theology, I am persuaded that infant baptism is the biblical view by inference. I also believe that the implications that favor infant baptism are overwhelming. Obviously, if I did not believe that, I would not espouse infant baptism.

Let us look at a survey of the arguments that are usually cited by those on both sides of this issue. First, we will review the traditional or classical arguments for baptism of believers and believers only. I will then explore the responses to those arguments and the other evidence that is often cited by proponents of infant baptism.

The major arguments against infant baptism include the following:

First, since baptism is a sign of the faith of the person receiving the sacrament, only those who possess faith (or at least profess it) should receive the sacrament. This is one of the chief reasons why

Baptist churches will not baptize infants. They ask, "How can you give a sign of faith to someone who is incapable of faith?"

Second, there is a sense in which the mandate to baptize is linked to repentance and belief in the commands of the New Testament. Proponents of believers' baptism note that the New Testament command to be baptized is articulated in these terms: "Repent and be baptized" or "Believe and be baptized." Opponents of infant baptism point out that a very young child is not capable of exercising repentance and faith because these are, at least in part, cognitive functions. Therefore, they say, young children should not be granted baptism.

Third, there are no examples of infant baptism in the New Testament. There are twelve examples of baptisms in the New Testament, but all of them involve adults and a prior profession of faith. In other words, the examples we see in the New Testament are of believers' baptism.

Fourth, early church historical records do not mention infant baptism until the middle of the second century. In other words, church history is absolutely devoid of examples of infant baptism until around AD 150, which is quite removed from the early church.

Fifth, the New Testament mode of redemption breaks down the Old Testament focus on ethnic continuity and biological inheritance. According to this argument, the practice of circumcision in the Old Testament communicated the principle of ethnic separation because redemption was accomplished through a nation of people by biological inheritance. When the New Testament era began, God's people were sent out to a Gentile world encompassing many different kinds of communities—a very different situation. Therefore, the method of redemption changed from biology, if you will, to theology.

There are also some secondary considerations on this side of the issue. Opponents of infant baptism argue that when the church baptizes infants in whom no regeneration has occurred, people become confused and may conclude that baptism transmits regeneration. They also say that while there are parallels between circumcision and baptism, there is no one-to-one correspondence or identity between them. Finally, as I previously mentioned, baptism as an adult experience is existentially more vital than that of an infant, who is not aware of the experience when the sacrament is presented.

These, then, are some of the arguments and concerns of Christians who do not engage in infant baptism. However, the negation of infant baptism, as a matter of historical record, is a minority report. That is, an overwhelming majority of churches historically have favored infant baptism. It is the historical perspective of Roman Catholics, Lutherans, Episcopalians, Presbyterians, Methodists, and many others. That in no way proves the validity of infant baptism, but those who hold a minority report should at least be willing to ask why their view differs from that of the vast majority of churches historically. They should be aware of the reasons churches that practice infant baptism do so, even if those reasons seem fallacious or invalid.

With that said, let us turn our attention to the ways in which proponents of infant baptism respond to the opponents, and to the evidence usually cited for this position. Proponents of infant baptism say the following:

First, the Old Testament sign of faith, circumcision, was given to infants, so the New Testament sign of faith, baptism, should be given to infants as well.

While proponents of infant baptism do not see an identity, an exact parallel, between circumcision and baptism, they do see this significant point of continuity: both circumcision and baptism are signs of God's covenant. Circumcision clearly was the sign of God's covenant in the Old Testament era: "And God said to Abraham, 'As for you, you shall keep My covenant, you and your descendants after you throughout their generations. This is My covenant which you shall keep, between Me and you and your descendants after you: Every male child among you shall be circumcised.... He who is eight days old among you shall be circumcised'" (Gen. 17:9–12a).

The Genesis record goes on to say, "So Abraham took Ishmael his son, all who were born in his house and all who were bought with his money, every male among the men of Abraham's house, and circumcised the flesh of their foreskins that very same day, as God had said to him" (v. 23). Later, after Isaac was born, "Abraham circumcised his son Isaac when he was eight days old, as God had commanded him" (21:4). Abraham was faithful to give the sign of the covenant to all the males in his family, just as God commanded.

Whatever else circumcision symbolized, it clearly symbolized faith. Abraham believed, and after he had faith, he received the sign of that faith. In other words, he received "believers' circumcision." But not only did he receive the sign of faith; he was commanded to circumcise his children; they also received the sign of the covenant and all it involved. As a result, Isaac was circumcised when he was only eight days old—he received "infant circumcision," the sign of faith.

Agreement is overwhelming that circumcision was the sign of the covenant in the Old Testament era. Everyone agrees that infants in the Old Testament were given the sign of the covenant. They do not agree, however, that infants in the New Testament era should receive the sign of the covenant. Our Baptist friends ask how it can be proper to bestow the sign of the covenant, which is also the sign of saving faith, upon someone who does not possess and is not even capable of possessing the gift of faith that the sacrament signifies.

If, however, a principle objection is raised to giving a sign of faith to someone who is not yet capable of demonstrating or exercising faith, then Old Testament circumcision must be condemned also. If it is wrong at all times and in all situations to administer a sign of something that is not yet present, the circumcision of infants in the Old Testament was wrong. So, the argument in Baptist circles proves more than it wants to prove. Baptists cannot object to the giving of the sign of faith to an infant now without being against the giving of the sign of faith to an infant at any time in history. Thus, they find themselves in contention with God in the Old Testament, for He clearly commanded that infants be given the sign of faith.

The real question is whether the practice of including children of believers as recipients of the sign of the covenant carries on into the New Testament period or whether it was annulled by the new covenant. That is the ultimate issue. Circumcision was a sign of faith that was given to infants clearly and explicitly. That is not a matter of inference; circumcision was commanded by God. But if circumcision was a sign of faith and of the fruits of faith, including salvation, would not God not only allow, but also command and insist, that children of the covenant continue to receive the sign of faith?

Second, although it is true that New Testament baptism is clearly linked to repentance and faith, that has no bearing on infant baptism.

As I noted earlier, when baptism is commanded in the New Testament, the mandate is "Repent and be baptized" or "Believe and be baptized." We find this mandate in the narrative passages, such as those in the book of Acts, where the New Testament records for us the Apostolic process and proclamation. The Apostles went about preaching, calling people to repent or believe, and then to be baptized.

Opponents of infant baptism cite this fact to argue that baptism should not be administered where repentance or belief has not occurred. They hold that, since there is no clearly taught exception for children in the New Testament, the formula "Repent and be baptized" or "Believe and be baptized" must apply to everybody, adults and infants alike. However, the Apostles were not addressing infants when they commanded their hearers to "Repent and be baptized" or "Believe and be baptized," for infants manifestly cannot repent or exercise belief.

Every church I know of that teaches and practices infant baptism also teaches and practices adult baptism or believers' baptism. If a pagan comes to a Presbyterian church and asks to be baptized as an adult, we are not permitted to baptize that adult until he or she has repented publicly and has made a profession of faith. Everybody agrees that, in the case of adults in the New Testament, the procedure is to repent or believe, and then to be baptized.

This also was true in the case of circumcision for adults in the Old Testament. Even then, adults had to make a profession of faith to receive the sign of faith. But infants in that era, just as in New Testament times, could not make a profession of faith, yet they were given the sign of faith. Therefore, it seems that infants in the New Testament era should also be given the sign of faith, baptism.

Third, while it is true that there are no explicit New Testament examples of infant baptism, there is Scriptural evidence for baptizing infants.

The absence of explicit examples of infant baptism in the New Testament is strange indeed. However, infants may have been included in some of the baptisms that are recorded for us. Twelve incidents that involve the baptism of people are recorded in the New Testament. Nine of these incidents clearly involve only adults, but three of them make mention of "households." The records say, "So and so and his household were baptized" (see Acts 16:15, 33; 1 Cor. 1:16). What does this mean?

Oscar Cullman, the Swiss New Testament scholar and theologian, argued that the Greek word *oikos*, the term that is translated "household," not only *may* refer to children but specifically *does* refer to children. We do something similar. If I were to speak of "John Doe and his family," would you think that John is married and has no children? The term *family* suggests children in addition to the spouse. The *oikos* formula is at least as weighty as our word *family*. The fact that households are mentioned does not prove that infants were baptized, but it at least favors the possibility that they were included.

There is another significant point to be made about the New Testament household baptisms. In the Old Testament, when the head of the family entered a covenant, his entire family received the benefit, and this covenant principle is reaffirmed in the household baptisms. That is significant—particularly since there are New Testament passages that specifically refer to infants and their status in the covenant. This is one of the most poignant arguments for infant baptism, though it is a reason that is rarely mentioned.

In 1 Corinthians 7:14, the Apostle Paul wrote, "For the unbelieving husband is sanctified by the wife, and the unbelieving wife is sanctified by the husband; otherwise your children would be unclean, but now they are holy." That raises questions for many people because we normally use the term *sanctified* to refer to the process that follows justification. Being sanctified presupposes being in a state of salvation. However, Paul, who elsewhere emphasized that salvation depends on faith, was not dealing with questions of justification here. He was speaking of how the power of God working through a Christian can influence that person's unbelieving spouse. But for our discussion of infant baptism, the important part of this text is the latter part. Why did Paul say that the unbelieving husband is sanctified by the believing wife? What is the reason? "Otherwise your children would be unclean, but now they are holy."

There are three words in this text that are very significant and pregnant with meaning: *sanctified*, *unclean*, and *holy*. What did these terms mean to a first-century Jew? In our doctrinal language, we use the word *sanctification* to refer to the process of being conformed to Christ after we are justified. But the primary meaning of *sanctification* in the Bible is to be set apart, to be consecrated, to be placed in a sacred favorable position, just as Israel was set apart from the "unclean" nations and declared to be a holy people.

The word Paul used for "children" is also very significant, for it specifically refers not just to children in general but to infants. He was saying that if at least one spouse is a believer, there is a certain sense in which the unbelieving spouse is considered sanctified—not for the sake of the believing husband or the believing wife, but specifically for the sake of the infant, that the infant may not be considered unclean but may be considered holy.

I submit that this is covenant language par excellence. Paul said that, in light of the language of the Bible, infants clearly belong in the new covenant, because the validity of the sacrament rests on the integrity of the One whose sign it is, namely, God.

Based on the New Testament, there is no doubt that our children have covenant privileges. The whole question then becomes if they are included in the covenant, why would they not be given the sign of the covenant? The sign of the covenant was given to infants in the Old Testament to show they were included in the covenant. If God were going to stop including infants in the covenant community, He undoubtedly would make it plain. The Old Testament laws that have been abrogated were abrogated by specific new teaching in the New Testament.

The biggest problem Baptists have is the silence of the New Testament. They want to argue that a principle that God initiates and maintains throughout the whole of Old Testament redemptive history suddenly is set apart in the New Testament, set aside without a word. It is supposedly repealed, and yet nothing is said about it. I submit that 1 Corinthians assumes the continuity of the inclusion of infants in the covenant.

The book of Hebrews labors the point that the new covenant is more inclusive than the old covenant, not less. If, under the new covenant, the infant children of the people of God do not receive the sign of the covenant that was given for thousands of years in the old covenant, then the new covenant is less inclusive, not more so.

Fourth, after the initial silence in the historical record, the practice of infant baptism appears to have been very widespread.

It is true that we have no surviving extrabiblical information that mentions infant baptism until the middle of the second century. However, when infant baptism finally is mentioned in the middle of the second century, it is spoken of as the universal practice of the church. It appears to be occurring everywhere.

It is possible to jump to the conclusion that the early church departed from the believers' baptism taught by the Apostles and started the heretical practice of baptizing infants, and that within a hundred years this heresy spread throughout the whole world. Yet, there survives an abundance of written material from Apostolic times to the middle of the second century that focuses on every serious controversy and theological debate of that period. Nowhere in all that material is there a word of debate about infant baptism. The historical record seems to suggest that this practice spread to become the universal practice in the church, and no one challenged it.

The reason for that appears to be obvious. At that time, the New Testament Christian community was much more in tune with the historic continuity of the covenants, and no one questioned giving babies the covenant sign. So, the argument from history is also in favor of infant baptism, not against it.

Fifth, the New Testament makes clear that people in the Old Testament were saved in the same way they are saved after the coming of Christ.

I once heard a learned theologian say that, in the Old Testament, redemption was transferred through biological descent, but that practice shifts in the New Testament. As noted above, opponents of infant baptism point to this apparent change and argue that circumcision was a mark of ethnic identity, so such a mark is no longer needed.

The New Testament makes clear that parental generation and propagation of children does not guarantee anyone's salvation. Even a person who is baptized and has parents who are Christians has no guarantee of being a Christian and being in a saved posture. The New Testament makes it abundantly clear that salvation is not ethnically or biologically inherited.

The New Testament makes it equally clear that such was also the case in the Old Testament—no one was saved because he or she was a child of Abraham or a child of Isaac. That was the heresy of the Pharisees, who believed they were automatically included in the kingdom of God because they were biological children of believers.

These major responses and arguments of proponents of infant baptism make a very strong case for this practice in the life of the church today.

The Baptist community says: "R. C., you build much of your case on the continuity between circumcision and baptism, between the old covenant and the new covenant, but the old covenant is not the same as the new covenant. Circumcision and baptism are not identical." I agree that they are not the same. There is an element of discontinuity between them. They are not identical, but they are not radically discontinuous. They are not radically different. They have a wealth of things in common, the most significant being that both of them are signs of the covenant of God with His people, and both are signs of faith. The debate is about where the discontinuity lies.

The challenge to the Baptists is that if they want to say that the new-covenant sign is discontinuous from the old-covenant sign on the critical point of the inclusion of infants in the reception of the covenant sign, then the burden of proof is on them. They must show us that the New Testament in fact departs from that which was the commanded practice of God. It was so important to God in the Old Testament that the infant children of His people receive the covenantal sign that He threatened to execute Moses when Moses delayed giving the covenant sign to his children (Exod. 4:24–26). In other words, in the Old Testament it was extremely important that infants received the sign of the covenant. If God does not change that explicitly, my assumption is that it remains important.

CHAPTER 9
THE LORD'S SUPPER

Early in my ministry, I took a bus from downtown Pittsburgh to Beaver Falls, Pennsylvania, where I was to speak at Geneva College. It was a bleak winter day. The bus traveled through one depressed steel town after another. The snow on the ground had turned black from soot and coal dust. As I passed through these towns, I observed the people getting on and off the bus. Many seemed to be out of work or elderly. They did not walk with a spring in their steps. Their pain and sense of hopelessness were written on their faces and in their gaits as they moved about. There seemed to be a pall in the atmosphere in these depressed towns.

As I was thinking these thoughts, I began to gaze out the window of the bus, and I realized that I could not go a city block without seeing a particular symbol. I would see it in the window of a storefront church or on the steeple of another church. It was the sign of the cross. I began to take heart from that. I realized there was still a visible symbol of hope for these people. Even amid the depression of their life situations and the encroaching secularism in the United States, the memory of Christ had not been eradicated. It was visible everywhere.

Then I thought, "As I am sitting here on this bus, somewhere in the world right now people are gathered together to break bread and drink wine to remember the death of Christ." I realized that with every second that passes on the clock, somewhere people are gathered to remember that moment in history when Christ was lifted up on the cross to pour out His life for our sins.

As we continue to examine the signs and symbols that God has given to His church, we come to the second of the two Protestant sacraments, the Lord's Supper. I do not think there was anything more important to the worship of the Christians in the early Apostolic church than the celebration of the Lord's Supper. This worship element was directly and sacredly instituted by Christ Himself on the night He was betrayed. We remember that, before His crucifixion, Jesus made plans with His disciples to secure the upper room, where they would come together to celebrate the Passover. There they would eat the ritual meal designed to commemorate the night God passed over the homes of the children of Israel because of the blood on their doors, which led to their exodus from Egypt. God instructed the people to celebrate that event every year thereafter lest they forget it. Jesus was eager to celebrate the Passover with His disciples. He said, "With fervent desire I have desired to eat this Passover with you before I suffer" (Luke 22:15). But while celebrating the Passover that night, He revised the ceremony, giving His followers a new ritual by which they might remember His great work. Thus, throughout church history, the celebration of the Lord's Supper has been central to Christian worship.

However, there are few articles of worship about which Christians disagree more. That is not surprising. Anything that assumes this kind of importance in the life of the church will engender debate because people tend to argue about matters that are important to them. I prefer that they debate rather than be indifferent to something of this solemnity.

Historically, almost every church has agreed that the Lord's Supper has three points of reference with respect to time. We divide time into the past, the present, and the future. This threefold orientation can be found in the drama of the Lord's Supper. Two of these dimensions cause little debate, but the third has sparked widespread disagreement throughout church history. Let us consider these three dimensions, starting with the past.

Obviously the Lord's Supper is concerned about remembering something that took place once for all in time past. Often the words "Do This in Remembrance of Me" are carved into the wood of Communion tables. Jesus exhorted His disciples on many matters to be diligent in their learning and to remember the things that He had taught them. But it is as if the culmination of His teaching came in the upper room when He said, "Do this in remembrance of Me" (Luke 22:19b). Our Lord said, in essence, "What is about to take place is the acme of My mission. I am about to ratify a new covenant, and I am going to do it in My blood. I am going to offer the atonement by which redemption is secured for My people. Whatever else you do, do not ever forget this."

I often use an illustration that gets less penetrating as the years pass. I ask, "How many of you can remember where you were and what you were doing when you heard the announcement of the assassination of President Kennedy?" For those of us who were living at the time, that was a moment of national trauma that was so intense and vivid, it is etched in our memories forever. We can even recall many years after where we were and what we were doing when we heard the news. Jesus wanted His atonement etched on the memories of His disciples in just this way.

So, a major dimension of what takes place in the Lord's Supper is reflection on the cross, but we miss much of the meaning of the Lord's Supper if we restrict it merely to the remembrance of things past. There is also a future orientation to the Lord's Supper. This dimension gets less attention from the church than the others, and I am not sure I understand why.

The Lord's Supper, as it was initiated, looked not just backward but forward. Jesus said, "I will no longer eat of [the Passover meal] until it is fulfilled in the kingdom of God" (Luke 22:16). The New Testament views that statement as pointing forward to the grandest feast of all history, the marriage banquet of the Lamb, when Christ will receive His bride and render her without spot and wrinkle, and will once again invite her to feast with the King (Rev. 19:7–9a). Therefore, every time we celebrate the Lord's Supper, we think about the past, and we remember that there is a future for the people of God; that we are having a foretaste at the Lord's Table of that ultimate fellowship we will have with Him in heaven.

Festo Kivengere, a tremendously gifted preacher, was a bishop in Uganda. He suffered greatly under the persecution of Idi Amin and had to flee for his life from that country. I heard the first sermon Festo preached in America. He preached the story of Mephibosheth, the son of Jonathan and grandson of Saul. Most of Saul's sons died with him in battle against the Philistines, and his son Ishbosheth was slain by two of his own men after a brief period as a pretender to the throne of Israel. Once David came to the throne, he wanted to honor his friend Jonathan, who had been killed with Saul. So, he said to his advisers, "Is anyone left of the house of Saul, that I may show him kindness for Jonathan's sake?" His secret service reported the rumor that a son of Jonathan had been secreted away and was in hiding somewhere in the kingdom. David asked that they ascertain his whereabouts and bring him to the palace. They found Mephibosheth, who had lame feet. Mephibosheth was terrified when he was brought to the royal court, for he thought David was planning to kill him. But David brought him to sit at the king's table every day so that he could honor him, not because of who Mephibosheth was in and of himself, but for the sake of Jonathan, Mephibosheth's father (2 Sam. 9). In his sermon, Festo said, "Brothers and sisters, who are we but spiritual cripples? We have no merit to commend ourselves to the unspeakable privilege of coming to the King's table; but because of the Father's love for His Son, we are invited to the King's house and to His table."

Since I heard that sermon, when I think about Mephibosheth, I think that what happened to him is exactly what has happened to us. Christ has directed the Spirit to go and search us out, and to call us for this future gathering at the Lord's Table.

There is not much debate about these two aspects of the Lord's Supper—the past and the future. Though there is great diversity in the church in terms of the methodology and frequency with which the Lord's Supper is celebrated, we all agree at least that there is a remembrance of something that happened in the past and an anticipation of something yet to happen in the future.

When it comes to the dimension of the present, there is more debate than I have space to cover in this chapter. The real question is about what happens now, when people gather around the Lord's Table and participate in this sacrament. What is going on?

Most of the debate centers on the somewhat enigmatic words that Jesus spoke to His disciples at the Lord's Supper when He changed the Passover feast into the new-covenant sacrament. He took the bread and broke it, and gave it to His disciples, saying, "This is My body which is given for you" (Luke 22:19). When they got to the point in the service where they drank the wine, He took the cup and said, "This is My blood of the new covenant, which is shed for many for the remission of sins" (Matt. 26:28).

Basically, the whole dispute focuses on the meaning of one word: *is*. What did Jesus mean when He said, "This *is* My body" and "This *is* My blood"?

The word *is* often functions as a copula, a linking verb. It is a form of the verb "to be." The verb "to be" can indicate identity. For instance, we say, "A bachelor is an unmarried man." There is an identification, a parallel, a symmetry between the subject and the predicate. But the verb "to be" also can indicate representation, and this is also true in the Greek language. In other words, it can mean "this represents or signifies something." When Jesus said, for example, "I am the door," He was speaking in metaphorical terms. No one interprets Jesus to mean there is an exact identity between Him and a wooden object that serves as a portal. We understand that He means He is like a door in some way.

We must ask: How did Jesus use the word *is* here? Is there a real identity between the bread and the wine and Jesus's body and blood, or is there simply a symbolic representation? There are almost as many answers to this question as there are churches, so I will give only a quick summary of the four major views of how Christ is present in the Lord's Supper.

The first, of course, is the classical Roman Catholic view of transubstantiation. In simple terms, the Roman Catholic Church teaches that in the Mass, during the prayer of consecration, a miracle takes place in which the common, ordinary elements of bread and wine are supernaturally changed into the actual body and blood of Christ. The result is that, at Communion, the person who is communing is actually participating in the body of Christ physically.

To understand the origin of this formula, we must look back to Aristotle's concern with the nature of substance. He said that every material object has two aspects—its substance (what it really is) and its *accidens* (what we call the outward, perceivable qualities).

The Roman Catholic Church sees a twofold miracle in transubstantiation. It holds that in the miracle of the Mass, the substance of the bread and the wine (the word *substance* is the root of the word *transubstantiation*) changes to the substance of the body and blood of Christ, although the accidens of bread and wine remain. For Rome, before the miracle, we have the substance of bread and the substance of wine, as well as the accidens of bread and the accidens of wine. It looks like bread; it tastes like bread; it sounds like bread if you drop it; it feels like bread; and it smells like bread—because it is bread. It does not look like someone's body, and it does not feel like someone's body because it is not someone's body before the miracle. Then the miracle takes place and the substance is altered. Now the substance of bread and wine is gone, and in its place is the substance of Jesus's physical body and Jesus's physical blood. All that is left of the original bread and wine is their accidens.

After this miracle, we have the accidens of bread and wine without the substance of bread and wine. There is also the substance of the body and blood of Christ without the accidens of the body and blood of Christ. When I say the miracle is twofold, I mean it takes a miracle to have the substance of one thing with the accidens of something else, and it takes another miracle to have the accidens of something and the substance of something else.

This is a very complicated way to define the real presence of Christ in the Lord's Supper. Though He cannot be seen, tasted, felt, or touched in terms of His accidens, Rome claims that the Communion partaker is actually chewing the body of Christ.

The second view is that of Martin Luther. He objected to transubstantiation because he felt it posited frivolous miracles. The Lutheran view historically has been called consubstantiation, although Lutherans characteristically do not like this designation. It is not their term.

On the one hand, Luther denied unnecessary miracles. On the other hand, he insisted on the substantial presence of Christ at the Lord's Supper. In colloquies and discussions on this, Luther behaved almost like Nikita Khrushchev at the United Nations, when

Khrushchev took off his shoe and pounded on the table over a particular point. When a great meeting of the Reformers was held to try to resolve differences over the Lord's Supper, Luther kept saying, with more and more gusto, "*Hoc est corpus Meum. Hoc est corpus Meum,*" which is Latin for "This is My body."

Luther insisted on this formula because he was very concerned people would trivialize the sacrament by reducing the elements to mere symbolism, empty or naked signs. He wanted to retain a significant doctrine of the real presence of Christ in the Lord's Supper. He said that Christ's substantive presence is in, under, and through the elements; that is, the substance of bread and wine is not obliterated by the visitation of Christ to the Lord's Table. The bread stays bread, and the wine stays wine, but underneath them, hidden from our view, is a real union of the body and blood of Christ with the elements. They remain imperceptible to us, but they are there. Christ is truly there substantially touching His human nature as well as His divine nature, so that we truly feed upon the body and blood of Christ in His glorified humanity at the Lord's Table.

The third view is that of Ulrich Zwingli, the Swiss Reformer, and for that reason it is called the Zwinglian view. This is probably the most widely held view among evangelical Christians today. It holds that there is no real substantive presence of Christ in the Lord's Supper; rather, the whole event is a sacramental drama wherein the elements remain mere signs and symbols. That is not to suggest that the bread and wine are not important signs and symbols. Zwingli said there is a representation of Christ in the bread and the wine, but there is no substantial presence of Christ's body and blood at the Lord's Table.

The fourth view, the Reformed view, was articulated by John Calvin. Interestingly, when Calvin debated Luther, he strenuously argued against the substantial presence of Christ in the sacrament, but when he debated with the Zwinglians, Calvin insisted upon using the word *substance* with respect to the presence of Christ in the Lord's Supper. Lest we think that Calvin was indulging in contradictions, we need to understand what he meant. The term *substance* can be used in two ways. It can be and often is used as a synonym for *physical* or *corporeal*. Thus, when Calvin spoke to the Lutherans, he denied the substantial presence of Christ in the Lord's Supper, by which he was denying the physical presence of Christ, the body and blood of Jesus. However, when he spoke with the Zwinglians, Calvin argued for the substantial presence of Christ, but in this instance he did not mean "physical" but, rather, "real."

Calvin declared that there is a real presence of Christ in the sacrament. Christ is really there at the table. We meet with Him in the sacrament and fellowship with Him in His real presence. But Calvin also said that the presence of Christ is in no way tied to the elements themselves. More significantly, he said that the physical presence of Christ is not immediately localized at the Lord's Table. So, the issue between Luther and Calvin was basically an issue of Christology. It had to do with how we understand the two natures of Christ.

At the Council of Chalcedon (AD 451), the church fathers made the statement that Christ is *Vera homo vera Deus*, or "Truly man and truly God." This is perhaps the greatest mystery we have to deal with in theology—how the human nature of Jesus can be perfectly united with the divine nature, and yet there is only one person. We do not know how this is possible, but Chalcedon affirms that the two natures are united, and that the union is without mixture, confusion, separation, or division, each nature retaining its own attributes. That is, when God in His divine nature unites with the human nature, the divine nature does not stop being divine; it does not give away its divine attributes. Conversely, when the human nature is united with the divine, the human nature does not stop being human. The two natures are joined but not confused.

For example, when Jesus wept, His tears were part of His human nature, because the divine nature does not have tear ducts, but the human nature does. Similarly, when Jesus was hungry, that does not mean that God got hungry. That was a manifestation of the human nature. We can distinguish between the human and the divine in this way, but we must remember that even when Jesus was hungry with respect to His humanity, His human nature was still perfectly united with the divine nature.

Earlier, when I mentioned my bus ride to Beaver Falls, I said that not a second passes on the clock without someone coming to the table somewhere in the world to celebrate the Lord's Supper. Is Christ present at each of those celebrations? To answer that question, we must answer this one: Do we believe that Christ can be at more than one place at the same time? The answer is yes; all Christians believe that. So, Christ can indeed be present each time the Lord's Supper is celebrated, and Calvin affirmed that He actually is present. But then we go to the next question, and we get a bit more technical. That question is, by what mode is He present? Is He able to be everywhere at one time in His human nature? Or, to put it another way, does the human nature of Jesus have the power or the capacity for omnipresence or ubiquity?

Calvin formulated this axiom, for which he is famous: *Finitum non capax infiniti*. It means, "The finite cannot contain the infinite." Calvin meant that, although Jesus's human nature is always and everywhere perfectly united with His divine nature, it is only the divine nature that can actually be everywhere at the same time. The human nature still retains the limits of humanness.

The Heidelberg Catechism states, in the answer to Question 47: "Christ is true man and true God. With respect to His human nature He is no longer on earth, but with respect to His divinity, majesty, grace, and Spirit He is never absent from us." This statement tried to do justice to Jesus's own teaching before He left this planet. On the one hand, Jesus said, "I shall be with you a little while longer, and then I go to Him who sent Me" (John 7:33). On the other hand, He said, "Lo, I am with you always, even to the end of the age" (Matt. 28:20b). Jesus announced a real departure and a real abiding. Therefore, historic Reformed theology says Jesus has departed in His human nature. His human nature is at the right hand of God in heaven, and we will not see that human nature again until He returns or until we go there. But in respect to His divine nature, Christ is still present with us.

We have a tendency to think that heaven is up there and earth is down here, and the human nature of Jesus is in heaven while the divine nature of Jesus is here on earth. However, that view results in the union of the incarnation being fractured. Calvin said the body and blood are up there because they are part of Jesus's human nature, which is localized. But the human nature up there is perfectly united with the divine nature, which is not limited to any one locale. So, the presence of Jesus Christ spans all of creation through the divine nature.

Calvin looked at it this way: when we celebrate the Lord's Supper here on earth, we are communing with Christ in His divine nature. Calvin said that in this act of mystical communion with the divine presence of Christ, the human nature of Christ is made present to us. In other words, when we meet at the Lord's Table with Christ through His divine nature, that nature is still in perfect union with the human nature. Therefore, we are communing with the whole Christ. It is not because His body and blood are brought to earth or our bodies and blood are carried to heaven. It is simply that in this intimate meeting at the Lord's Table, we commune with the perfectly united person of Christ, not just with His divine nature. So, even though we are apart from the human nature of Jesus, we really commune with Him in His human nature. This view keeps the human nature human and the divine nature divine, and strongly emphasizes that we truly are communing with the real presence of Jesus Christ at the Lord's Supper.

What, then, is the difference between that communion and the communion and fellowship we enjoy with Jesus in a Bible study, a prayer meeting, or any gathering of two or more believers? Could not we say that all of this is true in those contexts, too? In one sense, the answer is yes. Christ's presence is Christ's presence. The difference lies in what is happening in the differing contexts.

When I lived in Pennsylvania, I belonged to Latrobe Country Club. It was Arnold Palmer's club. I met him a number of times. Often I would be on the golf course at the same time he was, or we would be in the dining room at the club at the same time. But I was never invited to his house for dinner.

In our human relationships, just sharing a meal together is significant. When people get close, they begin to visit back and forth in each other's homes for the intimate fellowship of meals. Jesus at the Lord's Supper is saying, "You are coming to My house for dinner, and I am going to give you that kind of concentration of intimacy and assurance that goes with it." In other words, we have a special relationship with Christ that the unbeliever does not experience, because the Lord's Supper is for believers only. Nonbelievers can participate in our worship services, but they should not have access to the Lord's Table. That is where Jesus sits down with His people to give them special attention and to dispense a particular grace to them. He comes to comfort them, forgive them, and strengthen them.

We come to the table to see Jesus because we need Jesus to put His hands on our heads and forgive our sins. We need Jesus to give us a fresh assurance of our relationship with Him. When I take the bread during the Lord's Supper, it is as if I am hearing Jesus say, "R. C., I died for you; My body was broken for you, and My blood was poured out for you. I am stooping down in My grace to strengthen your soul this morning." It is an incredible experience.

So, I am not just thinking about the past or about the future. I am thinking about what is happening right at that moment. He is really there, we are in His presence, and we are being strengthened by this bond and communion of our souls with the presence of Christ.

CHAPTER 10
THE WHOLE PERSON

When pollsters ask people why they go to or stay away from church, the polls usually reveal the same thing. The number one motivation people give for going to church is the desire for human fellowship. They want to be with other people in a particular activity. Conversely, the biggest complaints from people who have dropped out of church—the main reasons for not attending—are that worship is boring and irrelevant and that the people at the services are not friendly.

We all know the number one reason we ought to go to church, and that is for the purpose of worshipping God. However, there are few of us, if any, who go to church exclusively for that reason. We go to enjoy the fellowship of our friends, to experience the expression of the symbols of our faith, and for other reasons. In fact, churches often try to appeal to these motivations. For instance, it is not uncommon for a church to design its building to communicate that this is a warm, comfortable, functionally convenient place to assemble together with one's friends.

Let us go back to the main reasons people cite for leaving church. They say that what goes on at church is boring and irrelevant. I have trouble understanding that. When we open the Bible and read the record of people who had encounters with the living God, we see the whole gamut of human emotions. Some people weep, some people cry out in fear and terror, and some quake and tremble. Abram fell on his face (Gen. 17:3), the Israelites "trembled and stood afar off" (Exod. 20:18b), and Isaiah cried out, "Woe is me, for I am undone" (Isa. 6:5a). There is a variety of responses to the presence of God, but we never read in the Bible of an occasion when God appears to the people and they are bored. Neither do we read of anyone walking away from an encounter with God, saying, "That was irrelevant."

A Christian service of worship is a gathering of God's people in His presence; it is an encounter with God. So, how can we account for the results of the polls that tell us that people come away from church feeling that it is boring and irrelevant?

I believe it is because they have no sense of the presence of God when they attend worship. The real crisis of worship today is not that the preaching is paltry or that it is too drafty in church. It is that people have no sense of the presence of God, and if they have no sense of His presence, how can they be moved to express the deepest feelings of their souls to honor, revere, worship, and glorify God?

The problem, of course, is in the use of the word *sense*. People have no sense of God because they cannot sense Him when the church gathers to worship. But if I said to you, "Next week at eleven o'clock in the morning, God the Father Himself is going to appear, visibly, at such-and-such a location, and we are selling tickets," would you buy one? Or if I said, "Jesus is coming back next week, and He is going to appear visibly in such-and-such a building at such-and-such time," would you go? If I told you that you had a chance to see God or Jesus with your eyes, you would not care what the building looked like. If you knew the Father or Jesus was going to be there, you would go. And if the Father actually showed up, or if Jesus visibly, physically came to worship, how many people do you think would walk away from that experience and say, "I was bored to death," or "That was irrelevant"? It is inconceivable that anyone would react that way to an experience of meeting with the Father or the Son.

Of course, the struggle to gain a sense of God's presence is not a new phenomenon. People throughout history have lacked a sense of His presence, and that often leads to the creation of images and idols, which are viewed as visible and tangible manifestations of God. Idolatry is simply an attempt to make God visible in ways that are unacceptable to Him. In a real sense, these attempts to gain a sense of the presence of God were simply earlier expressions of the kinds of experimentation we see in the worship of Protestant churches today.

John Calvin was keenly aware of God's prohibition against images in worship, particularly the second commandment: "You shall not make for yourself a carved image—any likeness of anything that is in heaven above, or that is in the earth beneath, or that is in the water under the earth; you shall not bow down to them nor serve them" (Exod. 20:4–5a). For this reason, Calvin called the church to examine its worship practices for improper use of images. It has been said, and I think fairly, that Calvin perhaps was driven more by a concern for proper worship than by theology in his work of Reformation in the sixteenth century (although, when it comes to Calvin, we can never really separate worship from theology). Whether that assessment is true is beside the point, but it is certainly true that Calvin was profoundly concerned with worship, and his biggest concern was the intrusion of forms of idolatry into worship.

Idolatry frequently made its entrance into the life of the church through the use of icons, images, and statuary. Because of this, Calvin had an ongoing debate with the Roman Catholic authorities about the use of these accoutrements in worship. The authorities in Rome made it clear that they prohibited the worship of icons, images, or statues in the Mass or in any form of religious activity. In saying that, they made a distinction between what they called *latria* and *douleia*—*latria* being the Greek word for "worship" and *douleia* being the Greek word for "service." Rome said we offer *douleia*, or service, to icons, images, and the statues, but never *latria*, or worship. Even Mary is not to receive *latria*, but she receives, as Rome said, hyper-*douleia*, or hyper-service.

Calvin claimed that this was a distinction without a difference. He said that to offer "service" to icons, images, or statues was, in effect, to engage in a subtle form of idolatry. To make absolutely certain the church would not be enticed or seduced into idolatry, Calvin wanted to clear all icons, images, and statuary from the house of God in worship. That became, for the most part, the stance of later Reformers. Even today, many who worship in the Reformed tradition tend to strip worship of visual dimensions.

The question of images in worship is part of the broader debate and controversy over what is proper worship before God. Some churches take the position that anything that is not prohibited in Scripture is acceptable for use in the worship of the church. Other churches have a principle that governs worship: the regulative principle. It says that only that which is authorized by Scripture is legitimate as a form of worship. (However, there is a great debate about what it means to say that Scripture authorizes something. Must Scripture authorize something explicitly, or can something be deduced by reasonable inference from the text of Scripture?)

This controversy has caused many of us to practice the philosophy of the second glance, that is, to look again to the Scriptures to discern, if possible, what principles we can find there that would lead us and guide us in our worship, and, at the same time, restrict us from a godless type of experimentation in order to achieve a sense of the presence of God. That is what I am trying to do in this book—find Scriptural principles that should inform our worship.

In my search for such principles, I keep going back to the Old Testament for this reason: in the Old Testament, I can find a refuge from speculation, from human opinion, and from tastes and preferences, because only in the Old Testament does God Himself explicitly demand that certain things take place in worship. In the Old Testament, God gives detailed instructions for worship. The Old Testament contains detailed passages prescribing how worship should be, but there is nothing like that in the New Testament.

This is dangerous ground, because, as I noted in earlier chapters, we cannot go to the Old Testament and transfer the liturgy of Israel and the forms of Jewish worship over into the New Testament. If we did that, we would be resurrecting the shadows and the types to replace the substance of the fulfillment of those things. In fact, the New Testament teaches us that the sacrificial system that was so much a part of the liturgy of Old Testament Israel is no longer to be repeated because it was fulfilled once and for all with the sacrifice of Christ on the cross. I am not interested in simply transferring Old Testament worship into the New Testament community, but what I am trying to find is whether there are principles we can glean from the Old Testament *cultus* of Israel that might have valid application in New Testament worship.

Jesus defined true worship for us in the New Testament when He said, "The hour is coming, and now is, when the true worshipers will worship the Father in spirit and truth; for the Father is seeking such to worship Him. God is Spirit, and those who worship Him must worship in spirit and truth" (John 4:23–24). Jesus's emphasis on truth certainly means that the mind must be actively engaged in worship. It is not to be bypassed or emptied in worship. Worship is not simply an experience of feeling; it must involve an understanding of the mind. That is why, in Protestant worship, so much attention is given to the reading and preaching of the Word of God. Preaching is designed, first of all, to appeal to the mind. Reading and preaching of Scripture are to be understood and subsequently acted upon.

The danger we face as Protestants is not so much the possibility of becoming mindless, although that is always there, but the real possibility that we might become Gnostics who think that our response to God is purely mental. We cannot let this happen because, when it comes to worship, the mind is not enough.

We can gain a better perspective on this matter by stepping outside the sphere of worship and looking at the broader question of epistemology, which is the science of how we learn or how we know anything. We understand that the learning process for every human certainly must involve the mind. If the mind is not engaged, we are not going to learn or know anything. However, we do not learn only through logical deduction.

René Descartes, the seventeenth-century philosopher, was concerned about the many conflicts of opinion in his time. He feared that truth was disintegrating. There was much skepticism and many collisions between various truth claims. In response, Descartes wanted desperately to find basic ideas, what he called "clear and distinct" ideas, that were so basic and foundational that their truth was indisputable. Descartes set himself to engage in a systematic process of doubt, whereby he determined to challenge every thesis he could possibly challenge until it could be proved compellingly and demonstrably that its truth was established by sheer logic. In this manner, he came to his primary truth, *Cogito, ergo sum*, which means "I think, therefore I am." He said that logic proves this beyond a shadow of a doubt. He said, in essence: "If I say, 'I am thinking and therefore I am,' if I doubt that, in order to doubt it, I have to be thinking. I cannot doubt without thinking. So, if I am doubting, I am thinking, and if I am thinking, I must 'be.' So that one thing I cannot deny is that I am thinking, and if I am thinking, I must be because I cannot have thought unless I am a thinker." With that, Descartes came to the conclusion that, given enough of these basic clear and distinct ideas, he could deduce the whole of reality without ever experimenting, observing, or measuring.

In truth, however, none of our experiences are purely cerebral or intellectual. Instead, the whole experience of human life involves the mental and the physical, or what I will call the sensate. The five senses are all involved in the experience of living. Those who are blind have a keen sense of the loss of one of their primary senses. Those who lose their hearing are often seriously disoriented because they can respond to life only by what they see, smell, taste, and touch. We are not creatures who experience the sum total of life with a bare-naked mind. Rather, we take it all by seeing, hearing, smelling, tasting, and touching. Recognizing this, the scientific method now puts most of its stress not so much on logic as on observation, the use of the five senses.

The senses are certainly important for us in any discovery of truth. One philosopher has said that we have no access to the world around us except through the senses. The body is the threshold of the mind for everything that exists outside of us. In other words, I cannot know anything is out there unless I see it with my eyes (or read about it), hear about it from someone, smell it, taste it, or touch it. Then the mind must process the information collected by the senses. To say that we learn purely with the senses and without the mind is as much of a distortion as saying that we learn or know purely with the mind apart from the senses.

The same is true in worship. We are not to approach worship as if we were disembodied minds. Neither are we to come to worship with skepticism, saying, "I cannot see God; I cannot hear Him; I cannot smell Him; I cannot taste Him; I cannot touch Him; and unless I can experience God with my senses, it does not matter what logic says to me, I will not believe that He exists."

When we study the worship practices God outlines in the Old Testament, we notice something very significant—the whole person was involved in the experience. The mind of the worshipper was engaged, as well as all five senses.

Along with Calvin, I realize that the Old Testament puts certain limits on how we can use our senses in worship. As already noted, God specifically prohibited graven images in the Ten Commandments, so dangerous was the peril of the intrusion of idolatry into the religious activity of Israel. Imagine if we were trying to formulate ten laws upon which to build a nation. Would we choose to use one of them to prohibit the making of images? Probably not, but the fact that God did so indicates the seriousness of the potential danger.

On the other side of the coin, there was a magnificent array of visual representations that was integral to the worship of Israel in the tabernacle and the temple. Israel's worship was intensely visual. Not only that, there was a strong element of auditory perception. Singing and instruments such as cymbals, trumpets, and harps were part of the experience of worship, not to mention hearing the Word read. There was an element of olfactory sense—the incense that was used to symbolize the sweet fragrance and aroma of the prayers of the people of God that rose before Him. Worship involved the whole person, including the senses.

For many years, I taught a seminary course on communication. About 80 percent of the course was devoted to the dynamic of verbal communication, but the remaining part of the course was concerned with nonverbal communication. Seminarians need to be taught about nonverbal communication because we tend to think that if we say the right words, we have communicated. That is not always the case.

In a theological discussion, my mind homes in on the words the other person is saying. I hear each word, and I analyze, to the best of my ability, the precise meaning of those words. I entered into a debate once with my mentor, Dr. John Gerstner. I protested against something that he said, and he turned my argument on its head, demolished me, and dusted off the spot where I stood. "But, Dr. Gerstner," I protested, "I did not mean that." He responded, "That is what you said, young man, and you're going to have to learn to mean what you say and to say what you mean." I was duly admonished at that point, and therefore I now try to think carefully about the words I select when I am engaged in theological discussion.

However, I do not always understand what the other person is really saying. When someone speaks to me, I listen to what he says, but if my wife is there, after the conversation is over, she is likely to say: "Honey, you completely missed that person's body language. You did not see the way he was frowning and the way his arms were gesturing. You have to be more holistic. You have to learn how to be more intuitive." My wife reads the person, whereas I am just one-dimensionally fixated on the words. I tend to miss all the nonverbal communication that is going on.

God uses nonverbal communication, especially in the context of worship. We see this clearly in the Old Testament worship instructions. The liturgy of ancient Israel clearly involved conceptual communication, but there was a strong element of nonverbal communication too.

THE WHOLE PERSON

In addition to involving the mind, Old Testament worship involved all five senses of the human experience, so that the whole person was engaged in this experience. God gave His people numerous worship elements that were designed to appeal to their senses. There were things to see, things to hear, things to taste, things to touch, and things to smell, and the same is true in the New Testament. In addition to the reading and preaching of the Word, we have singing and we have the sacraments, which appeal to nearly all of our senses.

We need to take a hard look at how we are engaged in the business of worship in terms of the whole person. Therefore, in the remaining chapters of this book, we will look at some of the elements of Old Testament worship that appealed to the various senses and consider whether we can use these elements to enrich our own worship. The place to start is with the visual dimension. What do we see when we are in the experience of worship?

CHAPTER 11
THE ROLE OF BEAUTY

When I was in the third grade, my grandmother took me to downtown Pittsburgh during the week before Christmas. We went to see the Christmas displays in the department stores, but also so that I could buy gifts for my family and, for the first time in my life, for a girlfriend.

I was filled with a sense of romance—at least as much romance as a third grader can muster. I selected a decorative pin. It looked to me as if this inexpensive pin were made of gold, and I had my girlfriend's initials engraved on it. I gave the gift-wrapped box to my girlfriend, and as she opened it, she giggled and exclaimed over the present.

I never really got over that experience because the gift I most love to give my wife of many years is jewelry. Almost every year, after

I have purchased her Christmas presents, I visit my friend Jack the jeweler and ask, "What are we going to do this year, Jack?" and he suggests various pieces of jewelry.

People of all civilizations and all ages have been fascinated with jewels because of their beauty. They become precious to us not because we can eat them or use them as tools, but because beautiful things can function as tokens that express love, value, and esteem. In other words, the giving of jewels can be a form of nonverbal communication.

When God told the Israelites to bring Him an offering for the construction of the tabernacle, He included jewels among the objects the people were to give (Exod. 25:1–9). These stones, and other valuable goods, would be used to build and furnish a place of worship that would be not only functional but also beautiful. God wanted His tabernacle to be aesthetically appealing.

In the last chapter, we discussed how Old Testament worship involved the whole person, both the mind and the senses. In this chapter, we will look at the visual dimension of worship. For those with eyesight, every worship service in the church has a visual dimension that is significant to the total experience, far more than many of us realize. We are creatures who respond to what we see with our eyes. We can walk into a church and see people bowing before statues, and that communicates something particular to us. We can enter an empty room with no pews, statues, tables, books, or carpeting. Even this empty space gives a visual experience. We cannot get away from it. Every building has some kind of form. It may be round or pentagonal. It may be shaped like a boat, as some churches are, or like a cross, as many churches are. It may have vaulted ceilings; it may have low ceilings. Every church building looks like something, and so, whenever we go to a worship service, we have a visual experience.

The principle is that every form we see is an art form, and every art form communicates something particular. For instance, everything that is manufactured by humans, no matter how simple it is, even a safety pin, is a certain color for a particular reason. The color communicates something. The color may not communicate anything dramatic, but it does communicate something. Visual response is important to human experience, particularly in terms of the worship experience.

Exodus 26 tells us about God's instructions regarding the construction of the tabernacle and its accoutrements. I do not think there is anything in Scripture to which God devoted more minute detail of description than the tabernacle. If ever God dictated any part of Scripture, it was when He gave these instructions. God revealed to Moses precisely how the structure was to look. He directly ordained and designed a place to be used for the purpose of worship.

When we look at the different forms of worship, all the liturgies devised by human beings, we respond warmly to some, while others leave us cold. I vacillate in terms of my evaluation of their validity or their lack of it. In Exodus 26 at least, we have a record of worship that was created, defined, and mandated by God Himself. Part of that is God's instructions for one of the two church buildings He designed (the other being the temple built later by Solomon).

Let us note the care that went into this. God said to Moses,

> Moreover you shall make the tabernacle with ten curtains of fine woven linen and blue, purple, and

> scarlet thread; with artistic designs of cherubim you shall weave them. The length of each curtain shall be twenty-eight cubits, and the width of each curtain four cubits. And every one of the curtains shall have the same measurements. Five curtains shall be coupled to one another, and the other five curtains shall be coupled to one another. (Exod. 26:1–3)

I am not suggesting that when we hang curtains in the church, that there must be exactly five curtains, four by twenty-eight cubits. This passage shows the infinite care that God gave to the accoutrements of worship in the Old Testament, down to the exact size of the curtains, the colors with which they were to be made, and the decorations that were to adorn them.

In Exodus 28, God gave instructions for the design of the garments of the priesthood of Aaron.

> Now take Aaron your brother, and his sons with him, from among the children of Israel, that he may minister to Me as priest, Aaron and Aaron's sons: Nadab, Abihu, Eleazar, and Ithamar. And you shall make holy garments for Aaron your brother, for glory and for beauty. So you shall speak to all who are gifted artisans, whom I have filled with the spirit of wisdom, that they may make Aaron's garments, to consecrate him, that he may minister to Me as priest. (Exod. 28:1–3)

Then God gave a detailed description of the ephod and the garments that were to be used by the priests. When God gave these instructions for the design and the manufacture of the robes and the clothing for the priesthood, He gave His reason for doing so. It was "for glory and for beauty." God was concerned that the priestly garments should communicate something about the glory and the beauty of God (Exod. 28:2b).

Again, we do not want to lift these instructions from the Old Testament and transport them over to the New Testament community because we would be reconstituting the Aaronic priesthood. To do that would be to deny the once-for-all finished work of Christ on the cross.

There is, however, a principle here with which we should be in tune. At least at this point in redemptive history, God was concerned that the experience of His people in their worship of Him would communicate His glory and His beauty, which the Old Testament repeatedly refers to as "the beauty of holiness" (2 Chron. 20:21; Pss. 29:2; 96:9). Whatever else the tabernacle and the temple were, they were magnificent works of art that bore testimony to God's glory and the beauty of His holiness.

The Christian faith emphasizes the good, the true, and the beautiful. It is clear that God is concerned about goodness because He is the fountainhead, the source, and the standard of everything that is good. As His people, we are called to mirror and reflect who He is, and so we are called to be good. Also, we understand from the Bible that there is a sanctity associated with truth because all truth ultimately comes from God. He is the essence of truth. But what about the third leg, the element of the beautiful?

One of philosophy's great questions is how objective norms for beauty are established. The science of aesthetics undertakes to study this. Is beauty purely subjective? That is, is it merely in the eye of the beholder? Or is there ultimately an objective standard for what is authentically beautiful and ultimately ugly? If we look to the Scriptures, we must come to the conclusion that there is an ultimate source of beauty, and it is the character of God. Just as God is the normative standard for the good and the true, so He is the ultimate standard of beauty.

God is clearly concerned about beauty, and we see this concern in the Scriptures. It can be seen in Revelation 21, where the New Jerusalem is described in all its splendor. It is in the language and the images used in the descriptions of Christ's love for His church and of the banquet feast in heaven, where Christ's church will be adorned as a bride is adorned for her bridegroom, without spot, blemish, or wrinkle. This describes a vision of loveliness. In heaven, the church will be beautiful, as well as good and true.

This same concern for beauty is seen in the Old Testament, including the instructions for the tabernacle we have been reviewing. God wants the worship offered to Him to be good—that is, holy— and not evil; true worship must be done righteously. Jesus told the Samaritan woman in John 4 that He wants worship to be in truth. God is not honored by heresy, false teaching, and lies. There must be a commitment to truth at the heart of our worship.

Even though we are far removed from the old-covenant ceremonies and rites, it appears to be consistent with the biblical pattern that we who live under the new covenant also should be concerned that our worship bear witness to the glory of God and to the beauty of holiness. It seems appropriate for our worship to be conducted in beautiful spaces with beautiful accoutrements.

The church once understood this better than it does today. As we have been discussing, the people of God in the Old Testament had a central sanctuary where all religious activity took place, but there was no focus on a temple or central sanctuary when the New Testament church began. As the church grew, buildings were established for people to meet for corporate worship. As Christians gave thought to the design of those buildings, a host of architectural forms developed, both in the East and in the West. Different traditions and patterns emerged. One of the most dramatic was the Gothic cathedral, with its flying buttresses, vaulted ceilings, and Romanesque arches.

I often ask my doctoral students, who are ordained and have ministered in the church for a while, whether any of them have been in a Roman Catholic cathedral. Most say they have, and I ask them to tell me their visceral reaction to that experience. Almost always the answer is along these lines: "I felt a sense of awe" or "I felt a sense of reverence." Sometimes they say, "At first I felt a sense of awe, and then I was brokenhearted when I saw all the trappings that are involved." I have to confess, I share those ambivalent feelings. Still, there is something about entering a Gothic cathedral that leaves a person acutely aware that a transition has been made from the profane to the sacred.

In St. Giles Church in Edinburgh, Scotland, there is an overwhelming sense of beauty. The stained-glass windows are some of the most magnificent in the world. They breathtakingly communicate something of the beauty of holiness, and there is nothing in them that involves images that may distort a person's understanding. St. Pierre's in Geneva is the church where John Calvin preached and taught every day. He was the Reformer's Reformer, a man greatly concerned with ridding the church of all aspects of idolatry. St. Pierre's is plain in terms of its ornamentation, but its architecture proclaims the transcendence of God. The design of the pulpit is especially magnificent. It is purposely placed forward, jutting into the congregation, so that it is not aloof or removed from the people. The form of that church communicates something of God's transcendent majesty. The same can be said for many other beautiful churches and cathedrals.

Such a structure was designed in the first place because the architect understood the principle that every form is an art form and that every art form communicates something. Whatever else was involved, the Gothic cathedral was built with the architect's intention to create a space to awaken a sense of the transcendence of God among those worshipping inside. And it worked. That is what people are responding to when they experience a sense of awe as they walk into a cathedral. They are impressed by the spaciousness, the height of the vault, the light streaming in. The whole accent of the building drives the human spirit to think in terms of the transcendent.

Architecture was not the only visual element God gave to His people. As discussed earlier, not only was the tabernacle beautiful, so was the clothing God designed for Aaron and his sons to wear while carrying out their duties as priests. The worshipper coming to the tabernacle had numerous reminders of the glory of God and the beauty of His holiness.

The Reformers, for the most part, were iconoclastic. There was a strong reaction against the liturgical system that had emerged after hundreds of years in the Roman Catholic Church, so many

Protestants disavowed any use of form or ornamentation in worship. They sought to rid church buildings of images, statuary, and other things that might entice people to become confused and get involved in idolatry. They adopted plain robes for their ministers.

As a result, we Protestants have tended to distance ourselves from anything that smacks of Roman Catholic tradition. For instance, generally speaking, churches now have moved in architectural design to create buildings that are designed for the comfort and convenience of the congregation. Fellowship is one of the reasons we come together every Sabbath day, so there is nothing wrong with having a building that accommodates that. Our buildings can be designed to facilitate human interchange. Buildings designed for that purpose, however, will follow a certain form, which will not communicate the glory and beauty of the character of God.

There are church buildings that are designed to give no hint of the building's true purpose as a house of worship. They are built to look more like town meeting halls. The chancel is no longer called the chancel; it is called the stage. The pulpit is not called a pulpit; it is called a lectern; and the congregation is not called a congregation, but an audience. Part of this is a desire to break through the old traditions that people have become inoculated against and no longer want any part of. In at least some cases, it is due to an abiding antipathy to beauty in worship, based on a desire to avoid an empty form of worship that is merely external. The church wants to exhibit that worship comes from the heart, not from external stimuli.

A crisis arises every time a congregation goes through a building program. Perhaps more people leave the church over the color the church basement is painted than over correct doctrine. Often, someone will say: "We shouldn't spend money on our sanctuary. It would be better to give it to missions or to feed the poor," and how can one argue with that? On the other hand, some say: "We want the sanctuary to be beautiful. We want it to be a place that expresses our desire to honor the magnificence of God." That, too, it a legitimate desire. This tension is always with us.

It is easy for us to make our churches and our sanctuaries not so much a reflection of our desire to honor God with beauty but rather an attempt to re-create the Tower of Babel and to build a monument to ourselves, to our affluence and our status. That is a precipitous danger any time we are building a church. So, we need to remember that when God built a church, He was concerned that it communicate not just His beauty but His glory.

No church going through a building project has unlimited finances, but new buildings do not have to be overwhelmingly expensive. Whatever we do, with whatever budget we have, should be done tastefully and with a view toward making the church building a visible expression of our desire to honor God—in the architecture and in the adornment. Everything ought to be weighed and considered, even down to the matter of whether the pastor should wear a robe and, if so, how it should look—for what he wears will have an impact on the worship experience of the people.

I sometimes wonder whether we are more concerned about our own appearances, decorating our own bodies and our own homes, than we are about honoring God in worship. This should not be. Our church buildings and our church services should be marked by visible beauty, so that we might be reminded of the glory and beauty of God.

CHAPTER 12

THE SOUNDS OF WORSHIP

I'll always remember the first time I heard the Westminster Brass ensemble. It was at the Philadelphia Conference on Reformed Theology many years ago at Tenth Presbyterian Church in Philadelphia. Today, it is commonplace to have brass ensembles in worship. At that time, it was very uncommon, and for the eight hundred or so congregants at the service, it was a radical innovation.

The opening hymn was Martin Luther's "A Mighty Fortress Is Our God." With the Westminster Brass providing the accompaniment, the people sang the hymn with gusto, and the service proceeded. Finally, the benediction was pronounced, and the Westminster Brass began to play the postlude. In many Presbyterian churches, the first strains of the postlude signal that the worship service is over and that people may leave. Something happened that night that I had never seen before. As the Westminster Brass began the postlude, no one moved. Everyone remained seated through the entire postlude. When the final strains were completed, this congregation of staid Presbyterians erupted in applause. They applauded not because they appreciated a musical performance. I wish I had the words to capture the atmosphere of that moment and the sense of worship that filled that church. Those Presbyterians, who were unaccustomed to this type of overt demonstration, applauded because they did not know what else to do; they did not know how else to express the depths of feeling they had experienced.

In this study of worship, we have been looking to the Old Testament to see whether we can learn from the patterns of worship found there. Again, I want to emphasize that we cannot reach back into the Old Testament and transfer ancient Israel's worship into the New Testament church. If we attempted to do that, we would be repudiating the fulfillment of the sacrificial system in the Old Testament that was accomplished by Christ. What we look for are principles of worship that possibly may be transferred from the Old Testament to the New Testament environment of the church.

I have noted that when God prescribed worship in the Old Testament, the whole person was involved. Not just the mind, but all five senses were involved in the worship experience of the people of Israel. These five senses, of course, are sight, sound, taste, touch, and smell. In the last chapter, we looked at how the sense of sight was involved in ancient Israel's worship. In this chapter, I want to consider the sense of sound.

Psalm 150 is the last in the book of Psalms. It is very short, only six verses. It begins: "Praise the Lord! Praise God in His sanctuary; praise Him in His mighty firmament! Praise Him for His mighty acts; praise Him according to His excellent greatness!" We see a repeated command to praise God, and we recall that the essence of worship is the offering of praise to God. This is underscored in Psalm 150.

But for our purposes in this chapter, I am most interested in the rest of the psalm, beginning in verse 3. Here the psalmist said:

> Praise Him with the sound of the trumpet;
> Praise Him with the lute and harp!
> Praise Him with the timbrel and dance;
> Praise Him with stringed instruments and flutes!
> Praise Him with loud cymbals;
> Praise Him with clashing cymbals!
>
> Let everything that has breath praise the Lord.
>
> Praise the Lord!

What can we infer from this psalm? Consider verse 3: "Praise Him with the sound of the trumpet." Does this statement mean it is possible to praise God with the sound of a trumpet? The answer is obvious—of course. If it were not possible, God would not command it. I doubt there is an easier inference from any biblical text than to infer from this text that, at one time in history, it was legitimate in principle to praise God with a trumpet. Since I cannot find anything in Scripture that contravenes this legitimacy, I must infer that it is still legitimate to praise God with the trumpet. We should never raise a principle objection against praising God with the sound of a trumpet. The same is true for the other instruments mentioned in this psalm. The psalmist said, "Praise Him with the lute and harp! Praise Him with the timbrel and dance; praise Him with stringed instruments and flutes! Praise Him with loud cymbals." Clearly, God sanctioned the use of many different instruments for worship.

There are, however, multitudes of professing Christians who are not familiar with Psalm 150. If asked, "What do you think about worshipping God with trumpets?" there would not be a unified response. In fact, there are churches that refrain from the use of any kind of musical accompaniment. There are groups of people within the church today that believe there is something inherently evil about using musical instruments in the context of worship.

For instance, I have been told that the only acceptable instrument to accompany worship is the organ or possibly the piano. But historically, what is the purpose of an organ or piano? In a symphony, unless there is an organ or piano solo, you usually do not hear an organ or piano played. Why, for the most part, is the piano or organ absent from the orchestra?

An orchestra is made up of a variety of instrumentation. There are string, brass, woodwind, and percussion instruments. The function of the organ, and to a lesser extent the piano, is to imitate the sound of an orchestra. The original reason organs or pianos were played in churches was because most churches were not large enough or wealthy enough to have an entire orchestra on the Lord's Day. It is interesting that people will say a piano is an appropriate instrument, but brass or percussion is out of place in worship. Psalm 150 indicates virtually all of the elements of orchestral music have God's sanction for worship.

The next question in terms of Jewish worship is what was the role of singing—the vocal and choral dimension of music? Singing of songs emerged very early in Israel's history. We read the song of Moses (Exod. 15), the song of Miriam (Exod. 15), and the song of Deborah (Judg. 5). Certain Levites who served in the temple did nothing but sing (1 Chron. 9:33). In the book of Nehemiah, we find that Nehemiah appointed choirs to celebrate the dedication of the rebuilt wall of Jerusalem (chap. 12). The psalms of the Old Testament are communicated not in the normal prose language but in metrical style, for they were meant to be sung. Clearly, singing was a vitally important part of the experience of worship for God's people in the Old Testament.

We also find singing in the New Testament. We know that Jesus and His disciples sang a hymn on the night He was betrayed (Matt. 26:30), and in the book of Revelation, we are told that in heaven, the Lord is going to give His people a new song (Rev. 5:9). Many songs were sung around the time of Christ's nativity as told in Luke: the *Magnificat* of Mary (1:46–55), Zacharias's *Benedictus* (1:68–79), the angels' *Gloria* (2:14), and Simeon's *Nunc Dimittis* (2:29–32).

Anthropologists and biologists tell us that human beings have an extraordinary capability of verbal communication, which is one of the distinctive things that differentiates humans from the animals. I have seen this through my experience of hunting wild turkeys. Turkeys have such precise eyesight they can see a person blink from a hundred yards away, so it is rare to walk up close enough to a turkey to shoot it. Therefore, a hunter must entice the turkey to come closer.

To that end, those who are dedicated turkey hunters practice for hours to learn how to call a turkey to their hiding places. The best turkey callers have been able to identify eight or nine distinct turkey calls. But compare that to human beings. When children begin learning to speak, they learn more than nine words or expressions a day. As adults, we have working vocabularies of thousands of words.

We can change the sound of our words, the intonation of our voices, and instead of speaking, we sing. We can say that God is like a mighty fortress or a bulwark that never fails, or we can sing that line from "A Mighty Fortress Is Our God." That is different from my normal manner of speaking. The mode of conveyance of the word is altered, and that makes an impact because when we sing or hear singing, something happens emotionally.

Simply put, when God created His people, He created them with not only the ability to speak but also the ability to sing. Knowing that we are to use every ability we have for God's glory and honor, we must use our voices in the service of praise and in the expression of worship that we offer to God.

Just as with the issue of instrumentation, there is controversy regarding the issue of singing in worship. The controversy erupts when we ask what types of songs are appropriate for use in the context of worship. Most of us would agree that what we want in worship is good music, not bad music. However, for some people, "good" music means classical and traditional music, while for others it means contemporary music.

It would be the nadir of arrogance to assume that all the good music, the kind that is suitable to be used in the church, has already been composed, and that only the innovations of the past are worthwhile for worship. We cannot determine the aesthetic value of music based on how long ago it was written or composed. It is also a mistake to think that the only good music is new music, and that if it is not new, it is not good.

It is instructive to remember that most of the hymns that are now well received in the church as part of the classic depository of hymnody were considered innovative at one time. In fact, many hymn writers borrowed from the musical styles that were popular in the secular world of their day, put them into a Christian context, and introduced them into the life of the church. In some cases, people raised objections to certain styles of music being used in the church. For instance, one of the most beloved hymn writers in fundamentalist circles, Fanny Crosby, consciously used the musical style that was popular in the bars of her day, and it was scandalous to people. It is an undeniable truth that when musical forms and styles change in the secular world, the new styles inevitably find their way into the church.

I visited a church a few years ago with a friend. When the congregational hymn was announced, it was one with which I was not familiar. As the congregation began singing, my friend whispered to me, "It is an all-skate." I knew instantly what he meant. In high school, I went to the skating rink and skated to the calliope or the organ music that was played for the accompaniment of the skaters. This hymn was reminiscent of the music used in the skating rink, and it had found its way into the church. So, the questions arise: Are certain styles of music inappropriate for use in worship? What really constitutes "good" music? What's the difference between a cacophony and a symphony, between a short-lived ditty and a musical piece that will last through the ages?

These are not easy questions to answer. There are those who think that a definition of beauty is utterly subjective, while others have sought transcendent norms, principles, and rules that define beauty—not just visual beauty but musical beauty. If we go back through the ages of the study of aesthetics, which is the theory of beauty, we find Aristotle, Thomas Aquinas in the Middle Ages, and Jonathan Edwards, who wrote a magnificent study of aesthetics, delving into that question. These men had certain things in common. They tried to isolate the elements that distinguish beauty from ugliness, and they listed criteria such as harmony, proportionality, and complexity as factors that can be used to judge the quality of all types of artistic compositions, including music.

In an art museum, invariably there are people seated on benches in the galleries, staring fixedly at particular works of art. In fact, I could be one of those people. I love to go to the Rijksmuseum in Amsterdam, Holland, where there is a large Rembrandt collection. I can look at paintings by Rembrandt for hours, and the more I look at them, the more I see in them. They never become boring because Rembrandt captured such depth on those canvases that they can keep the mind engaged for long periods of time. Rembrandt's paintings have a high degree of harmony, proportionality, and complexity, and for that reason they hold a person's interest. The same would not be true if Rembrandt had drawn stick figures. The quality would not be there, and they would not be interesting.

Judgments about quality tend to take place over time. When a new song is composed, there is a sifting process, and we eventually find out whether that song will stand the test of time. In the realm of popular music, there are many songs that were written in the

1950s or in the '60s that stayed at number one for weeks and then dropped from the charts, but they are still part of the music we call the "golden oldies." There are other songs that reach the top of the charts for six weeks and drop completely out of sight and mind, so that people today have never heard of them. The compositions being created today will all go through this sifting process of time. Some will vanish, but others have the majestic measure of beauty that will keep them around for years.

Even if a song is aesthetically beautiful, it still may not be appropriate for use in worship. That leads to one last element about music: the lyrics.

The issue of the lyrics used in songs of worship is no small problem. Much of the theology that is conveyed in the church is learned not by courses in the Bible or in theological instruction, but by osmosis from singing hymns over and over. Therefore, hymn lyrics can be helpful or harmful to people.

For the most part, the theology that comes to us in traditional hymns is outstanding. This was brought home to me when I received a card celebrating the birth of Christ. All the text of the card said was, "Far as the curse is found." That line, from the carol "Joy to the World," is preceded by the words "He comes to make His blessings flow ..." Those few words encouraged me to think about the scope of the redemptive ministry of the incarnate Christ, about the curse that fell upon the world until Christ came to bear that curse on the cross, and about the joy that emanates from the Christ child's birth extending as far as the curse extends. What a magnificent statement that is. When I sing that Christmas carol, I am reminded that there is a lot of good theology in many of our great hymns.

Unfortunately, there is also some bad theology in traditional hymns. Some older hymns used in the church today are simply heretical. Some hymns are sung in the church in a far different context from their intended meaning. Charles Wesley's hymn "Oh, Perfect Love" has been used as a wedding song, celebrating romantic love between two human beings, when the entire thrust of the hymn is about a love for God that is made perfect by the "second blessing" espoused by the theology of perfectionism. The theology of that hymn is on a collision course with orthodox Christianity. There are other songs that have statements in them that are simply unbiblical.

There is at least one denomination in the Reformed tradition that sings only psalms for Sunday morning worship. The believers in that denomination reason that the psalms were inspired by God, so there is no danger of bad theology in their words. They think that whatever we sing should be the Word of God. I do not think we need to go that far, but whatever we sing must be consistent with the Word of God. It should be theologically and biblically sound. Luther had Psalm 46 in front of him when he wrote "A Mighty Fortress Is Our God." He did not use the exact words from Psalm 46, but the content of the message of Psalm 46 forms the core announcement of that hymn. We need that kind of music for worship, songs with words that communicate biblical truth. The beauty of worship is never to be divorced from the truth of worship.

The thing I look for above all else in church music is the sense of transcendence. Music in worship should not familiarize God to me; rather, it should stimulate the soul to a posture of adoration.

One of the most popular praise songs of recent years is "Majesty." Its popularity may have something to do with the sound of the music itself, but the song also has wonderful words. Christians are hungry for a way to express a sense of the majesty of God. Good, biblically sound music is a marvelous enhancement to that end.

CHAPTER 13

THE TOUCH OF ETERNITY

We have looked at the Old Testament structure of worship and have seen that not only the mind was engaged in the experience of worship but all five senses: sight and sound, which we have considered already, and touch, taste, and smell, which we will cover in this chapter. First, the Scriptures make clear that God intended touch to be an important element of the drama of Old Testament worship.

As a graduate student in the Netherlands, I played baseball as a diversion from constant studying. The sports editor of a large newspaper in Holland asked to do a brief interview with me. I thought his interest in interviewing me about playing baseball was strange, but I agreed. The editor came and interviewed me; then a photographer took my picture. I expected the article would be buried somewhere in the back pages of the sports section. However, a few days later I saw a huge picture of myself on the front page of the sports section, along with a two-inch headline that said in Dutch, "American Minister Baseball Player." The editor's interview with me was the lead article for that day's sports page.

As I read the article, it suddenly dawned on me that the article had nothing to do with my prowess as a baseball player. What made me newsworthy was the fact that I, a minister, was sliding around in the dirt playing baseball in public. This was absolutely unthinkable in the Dutch culture, where everything to do with the church was highly formal.

At that time in the Dutch worship service, there was no processional. Rather, there was an opening hymn, and when it was time for the minister to start the service, he entered the sanctuary from a side door. Upon his appearance, the congregation stood, and when the minister sat down, the congregation sat. The minister preached in a tuxedo. After the benediction, everybody stood in the minister's honor, and he left, again, by the side door. We did not see him afterward.

This atmosphere of formality was a culture shock for me because our custom on Sunday in the American church was for the minister to personally greet the members of the congregation after services by shaking hands and having a short, cordial conversation. In the Dutch church, there was no contact with the pastor. That was considered an unnecessary social triviality.

In my estimation, the Protestant churches in Holland have suffered from that particular practice. Why do I say that? Some interesting studies have been made by doctors, psychiatrists, and psychologists about the importance of the human touch. It has been found that babies, if they are left in a hospital nursery and receive no human touch, can actually die. Human beings need to be touched; the human touch is extremely important, so important we long for it. This is an important aspect in the church, where the minister, as Martin Luther put it, represents Christ to his congregation. People longing to be touched by Christ need contact with their minister.

THE SENSE OF TOUCH

We read in the New Testament about the laying on of hands. This practice has its roots in the Old Testament in the anointing of people for particular ministries. The king was anointed by a prophet, who poured oil over the head of the new monarch. Priests and prophets also were anointed. The oil was poured on their heads to consecrate them, to set them apart for their sacred vocations. The outpouring of the oil indicated a transfer or an imputation of divine grace to an individual in order that he might be empowered for his office. It was a symbol for the transfer of power from God to a human being.

In the New Testament, the ordination of individuals for particular offices or tasks was accompanied by a similar practice—the laying on of hands. The church at Antioch laid hands on Paul and Barnabas before sending them off as the first missionaries (Acts 13:3). Likewise, Timothy apparently was ordained as a pastor through the laying on of hands (1 Tim. 4:14).

Today, most churches that ordain people to church offices, to the clergy, or to the eldership have some kind of service of ordination that involves the laying on of hands. In Presbyterian churches, the members of the presbytery come forward, gather around the ordinand, and lay hands upon his head as a symbol of the laying on of the hands of Christ, of the anointing of God. In Episcopalian churches, it is done by the bishop, but the purpose is the same. I will never forget my own ordination to the ministry, and I wish every Christian could experience the laying on of hands as I did on that occasion. The human touch I experienced on that occasion was precious to me.

We see the sense of touch addressed also in the matter of the benediction. When God gave His instructions for worship in ancient Israel, He commanded that the priest should pronounce a specific blessing over the people: "The LORD bless you and keep you; the LORD make His face shine upon you, and be gracious to you; the LORD lift up His countenance upon you, and give you peace" (Num. 6:24–26). Aaron and his successors as priest used these words to proclaim God's blessing on His people.

In the New Testament church, the bishop or presiding officer of the congregation made a similar pronouncement called a benediction. The prefix *bene* is derived from the Latin word that means "well," while *diction* is from the Latin word meaning "to speak," and so, a benediction is a "good saying." These early Christian services took place in house churches, and the congregations were small. The pastor blessed the congregants on an individual basis, and while he blessed them, he touched them. He laid his hands on them.

Over time, as the churches grew bigger, the practice of individual blessing had to be abandoned. The pastors blessed their people all at one time while facing the congregation with upraised hands, and that is how it is done in most evangelical churches today. The benediction that we pronounce today with hands uplifted is a symbolic expression of the minister touching his people.

THE TOUCH OF ETERNITY

Years ago, I spoke at a service at a large church in California. After I finished preaching, the associate pastor invited everyone who would like to have prayer to come forward to the long kneeling bench across the front of the sanctuary, and seventy-five or eighty people responded. The minister then gave a closing prayer, but as he prayed he walked along the bench and touched each person on the head very gently. I thought: "This is remarkable. This is a recovery, in a sense, of the ancient tradition of having a physical touch that is a part of the worship service."

Jesus understood the importance of touching those to whom He ministered. Very often, when He healed people, He touched them. We see a beautiful example of this in Matthew 8, where a man with leprosy approached Jesus to ask for healing. Leprosy was extremely contagious and was incurable, so those who contracted it became social outcasts, forced to live apart from the rest of the community. But Jesus not only healed the leper; He also touched the man. Jesus ministered to his physical need and to his need for human contact.

People today need that touch. That is why an important moment in church on Sunday morning is when the pastor interacts with the worshippers as they depart. I tell my students in the seminary that there is an art to greeting people at the door after the church service. It is vitally important for the pastor to extend his hand and at least offer to shake hands with every person who comes by. Some will walk right by, but the vast majority of people want to stop and shake the pastor's hand. If that person is an elderly man or woman, and especially if it is an elderly widow, the pastor should never, ever shake with one hand. He must take that woman's hand in both of his hands. Why? It is because she needs that special touch, because she experiences loneliness. In giving that tender, loving touch, the pastor is being Christ to the people, giving the Master's touch in His name to people who are afraid, lonely, or hurting. People want to be touched, not in an evil sense, but in a tender and merciful sense, in a human sense.

Every Christian would love to kneel in Christ's presence, feel the touch of His hand, and hear Him say, "Your sins are forgiven," or "Be healed and go in peace." He does not do that now, but in His wisdom God has made provision for people to be ministered to through touch as we worship together.

THE SENSE OF TASTE

God-designed worship also appeals to the worshippers' sense of taste. The sense of taste is highly subjective. We all like the taste of some things and dislike the taste of other things; we do not have a uniform agreement on that. But taste is powerful, and so there are constant references in the Bible to this aspect of our humanity, many of which are used in a metaphorical way.

The Bible says, "Oh, taste and see that the LORD is good" (Ps. 34:8a). That image, of course, is borrowed from the common human experience of tasting things that we experience as sweet and that we believe are delicious. By inviting us to "taste" a relationship with God and assuring us that we will find it "good," the psalmist makes his point in a powerful way that we all can understand.

In Bible concordances, there are dozens of references to the term *honey*. The Word of God is said to be "sweeter ... than honey" (Pss. 19:10; 119:103), by which we understand that God's Word is delightful and desirable. Very early in Ezekiel's ministry, God called the prophet to eat a scroll, and the words of the scroll contained an oracle of judgment in which God was announcing the outpouring of His wrath upon the nation. Though the message seemed bitter, when Ezekiel put the scroll in his mouth, he was astonished to discover that it tasted sweet, and he made the comment that it tasted as sweet as honey (Ezek. 3:1–3). Thus, we understand that even God's words of judgment are good.

In these references to taste, God taught His people certain truths in a metaphorical way. He did much the same by enshrining certain tastes in the worship He designed for His people. At His command, Israel kept frequent feasts to commemorate God's involvement with His people. These feasts were not potluck dinners. The contents of the meals were prescribed by God, and each element of the food and drink—the bitter herbs, the unleavened bread, the lamb, the wine— had symbolic significance. God saw a kind of continuity between the physical taste of these foods and drinks, which were common to the Jewish people, and real historical experiences. He wanted them to remember the bitterness of their stay in Egypt and the sweetness of their redemption that was accomplished in the exodus, so every year, the Passover was to be celebrated.

Today Jewish people still observe the Seder, the meal that was associated with the Passover feast (Exod. 12). They replicate the same menu from generation to generation so that certain foods and certain tastes are associated with the work of God and with the Word of God.

Christians no longer observe the Passover; instead, we celebrate the Lord's Supper. We looked at this sacrament of the church in depth in chapter 9, and we saw that as Jesus neared the end of His ministry, He longed to eat the Passover meal with His friends once more. In the middle of the Passover meal, He changed the liturgy, inaugurating a new covenant for His church. He took the bread, which already had been consecrated and was associated with the redemptive, historical act of Passover, broke it, and said, "This is My body, broken for you." He attached a redemptive significance to that symbol, the bread, and told His church to continue to eat it in remembrance of Him and of His work. When we celebrate the sacrament of the Lord's Supper, taste is involved. We taste of the bread of life.

Jesus also took the cup that held the wine, and He said, "This is My blood of the new covenant." John Calvin mused that wine is a remarkably suitable vessel of communication, for it tells us something about the atonement of Christ for us. Calvin noted that in the cultural history of Israel, wine was considered to have a bitter taste and to burn when swallowed, so it was used to remember the bitterness of the slavery the people experienced in Egypt. Yet wine was also used in a positive way for magnificent feasts and celebrations in Israel. The Bible says, "Wine ... makes glad the heart of man" (Ps. 104:15). There was also a long tradition in Israel of using wine to express joy and gladness in times of celebration.

Wine has this dual significance that seems, on the surface, to be contradictory. But Calvin said that dual significance made wine especially appropriate for remembering the Lord's death on the cross. For while the cross was the most bitter moment in human history, the most diabolical act ever committed, it was also the greatest moment in human history, the moment that effected our salvation, that gave grounds and cause for the people of God to rejoice.

Therefore, at the Lord's Supper, we remember the death of Christ in a kind of sober mourning, but we also anticipate the promised future of the people of God, when we will sit down together at the marriage feast of the Lamb with His bride. At that great feast, Jesus will be the host. We will sit down with Him and with Christians from the East and from the West, and we will enjoy unparalleled gladness. So, when we observe the Lord's Supper, we look backward to Black Friday, but then we begin to see that Black Friday was Good Friday, and we look forward to the fulfillment of joy that is stored up for us in heaven. All of this is communicated through the taste of these common elements.

There is an ongoing controversy in that many Protestant churches do not use wine in the celebration of the sacrament. In fact, I think the majority of churches do not use wine; most use a form of grape juice. One of the major reasons for that is the problem of alcoholism, and church leaders want to try to protect their people from unnecessary temptation. In other cases, churches do not believe Jesus used real wine. I agree with Calvin—real wine communicates to our taste buds both elements—pain and joy, sorrow and gladness—and somehow, in my opinion, grape juice just does not do it. I think we lose something if we do not use wine, because in the worship of Israel God associated certain truths with certain tastes.

THE SENSE OF SMELL

Finally, let us consider the role of the olfactory sense, the sense of smell, in worship. We Protestants give almost no consideration to this sense in our worship experience, and I believe that by failing to do so, we are impoverishing our worship; for the sense of smell is quite powerful.

Researchers tell us the human nose can discern several thousand distinctive aromas. Some are pleasant and some are unpleasant, but memories of fragrances tend to linger in our minds and provoke strong associations. For instance, when I smell hot dogs cooking, I think about being at a baseball park. Likewise, I love to walk into a bakery because the smell of baking bread invokes all kinds of memories of my aunt and of my grandmother baking in my home when I was a child. Who does not associate the scent of pine needles with Christmas? Popcorn suggests movies. Burning leaves suggest fall. There are innumerable scents that we associate with certain people, certain times of the year, certain places, and certain experiences.

God understands this human proclivity, so when He gave instructions for the tabernacle, He included an aromatic dimension. One of the pieces of furniture He commanded for the tabernacle was the altar of incense. The purpose of this altar was to symbolize prayer. We talked about the altar of incense in chapter 4, where we saw that John the Baptist's father, Zacharias, went into the temple to burn incense and pray to God as the representative of the people. The smoke from the incense rose up toward heaven, and that symbolized the rising up of the prayers of the priest and of the people to God. Zacharias used incense that had been prepared the same way for thousands of years, just as God commanded (Exod. 30:34–38). Over those centuries, the Israelites had smelled that unique aroma countless times, so they had come to associate that fragrance with the presence of God.

That symbolic element of worship in the Old Testament informed the mode of speaking and verbal expression in the Scriptures. For instance, when the Israelites would offer their sacrifices to God in the prescribed manner, God would speak of them as "a sweet aroma" (Exod. 29:18; Lev. 1:9). When God became angry at the Israelites for their apostasy and their hypocrisy, He said to them, "Bring no more futile sacrifices; incense is an abomination to Me. The New Moons, the Sabbaths, and the calling of assemblies—I cannot endure iniquity and the sacred meeting" (Isa. 1:13). God was saying, in effect, "Your offering has become a stench in My nostrils. Your praises stink."

In the New Testament, the work of Christ is pictured as pleasing and delighting the Father like a sweet fragrance (Eph. 5:2). So, too, is the work of the saints; our obedience is a sweet-smelling savor, a sweet aroma, a sweet fragrance to God (2 Cor. 2:14–16). All that language of fragrance was drawn from the worship experience of the people in the Old Testament.

There are very few Protestant churches that still incorporate incense in worship, and if you were to suggest it in your church, your suggestion might not be well received. Why is that? It has to do with the reaction of our Protestant forebears against the Roman Catholic form of worship in the sixteenth century. Because Rome used incense, the Reformers rejected it, and now we have, as it were, thrown the baby out with the bathwater. In our Protestant protest, we have isolated ourselves from an element of worship that God provided, and we have lost something.

We need to see that when God ordained worship, He included an olfactory dimension. Therefore, we have to be careful about making a principal objection to the use of incense in worship.

CONCLUSION

How then shall we worship? To honor God as God, we must worship Him as He, and He alone, decrees.

No church dare replace the chancel with a stage. Stages are built for performance; chancels are constructed for worship. We must work, and work hard, to remove the shadows we have placed over the glory of God, that God's people may be renewed by basking in His divine splendor and brilliant glory.

Nothing else will do.

ABOUT THE AUTHOR

Dr. R. C. Sproul is the founder and chairman of Ligonier Ministries, an international Christian education ministry based near Orlando, Florida. He also serves as co-pastor at Saint Andrew's, a Reformed congregation in Sanford, Florida, and as the president of Reformation Bible College. His teaching can be heard on the daily radio program *Renewing Your Mind*.

During his distinguished academic career, Dr. Sproul helped train leaders for the ministry as a professor at several theological seminaries.

He is the author of more than eighty books, including *The Holiness of God*, *The Work of Christ*, *Chosen by God*, *The Invisible Hand*, *God's Love*, *The Truth of the Cross*, and *Pleasing God*. He also served as general editor of *The Reformation Study Bible* and has written several children's books, including *The Prince's Poison Cup*.

Dr. Sproul and his wife, Vesta, make their home in Longwood, Florida.

STUDY GUIDE

CHAPTER 1

INTRODUCTION

We face a crisis of worship in the church. For decades we have sought to make worship feel more enjoyable and relevant, but many people still find it boring. One useful way to pursue truth about a subject is to dig down and look at the foundation upon which everything else is built. In seeking to find God-ordained principles for worship, the foundation is the form of worship laid out in the Bible. While there isn't 100 percent continuity between Old and New Testament worship, there are some extremely valuable things we can learn by looking back at that foundation.

LEARNING OBJECTIVES

1. To be able to explain why form in worship is necessary, and how it differs from formalism.
2. To be able to discuss some continuities between the Old and New Testaments, as well as some discontinuities.

QUOTATIONS

Hypocrites! Well did Isaiah prophesy about you, saying: "These people draw near to Me with their mouth, and honor Me with their lips, but their heart is far from Me. And in vain they worship Me."
—Matthew 15:7–9a

Let all things be done decently and in order.
—1 Corinthians 14:40

OUTLINE

I. Introduction
    A. There is a crisis of worship in the church today.
    B. Many people find church boring and irrelevant.
    C. The worship battle lines between formal and informal represent a false dilemma, because group worship always has some form—that is, an order or pattern.

D. Therefore, the real question is, "What will be the structure, the style, and the content of the liturgy [pattern]?"

E. To know whether the form we've chosen is legitimate, we need to search out what God has shown He wants us to do in worship. What pleases God is more important than what excites us.

II. Continuity and Discontinuity between Old and New Testaments

A. Vast portions of the Old Testament describe a practice of worship that God Himself ordained.

B. Much of that Old Testament ritual focused on the sacrificial system, which was fulfilled once and for all in the atonement of Christ.

C. If we insist on total continuity between the testaments, we may slip into the Judaizing heresy and deny the fulfillment of the covenant that Jesus accomplished.

D. However, we must also avoid the opposite error of thinking there is no continuity at all between the testaments.

E. Marcion was a heretic who taught that the God of the New Testament is not the same as the God of the Old Testament. He created an abridged version of the New Testament that left out all connections with the Old.

F. Few people today teach Marcion's ideas wholly, but his heresy lives on in the evangelical church's neglect of the Old Testament.

III. Antinomianism and the Crisis of Morals

    A. The neglect of the Old Testament has led to a moral crisis because of pervasive antinomian theology.

    B. *Antinomian* means opposed to the law of God, including the Old Testament law of God.

    C. Some Christians think that we are responsible to obey the commands of Christ but that the Old Testament law of God has no relevance to us. This is classic antinomianism.

IV. Crisis of Worship

    A. The neglect of the Old Testament has also undermined our worship, because we often behave as if nothing God said about worship in the Old Testament applies today.

    B. God did not dictate books like Romans word for word to Paul, but He did dictate to Moses His instructions for the form of Israel's worship.

    C. Although there are some important discontinuities between Old Testament worship and our own, there are principles in the Old Testament patterns that should inform our own patterns.

V. Form but Not Formalism

    A. All corporate worship has a form or pattern, but we must be careful not to let the pursuit of a proper form become an end in itself.

    B. At the time of the Reformation, the problem with Roman Catholic worship was not with the form of worship but with *formalism*, in which the form becomes the end in itself.

    C. A related term is *externalism*, in which the external elements of worship exist but the heart and soul are absent.

    D. The Old Testament prophets were reformers but not revolutionaries. They denounced not Israel's liturgies but the coldhearted worshippers who went through them by rote.

    E. Jesus, too, denounced externalism, not the liturgies God had prescribed.

    F. Our goal should be liturgy that is biblical in content and that helps us worship in spirit and in truth.

BIBLE STUDY

1. What do the following texts indicate about the continuities between the Old Testament and Jesus' teaching? What do they indicate about the discontinuities?
a. Matthew 5:12–20
b. Matthew 5:21–24

c. Matthew 22:34–40

2. Acts 21:17–26 describes Paul participating in the rites in the Jewish temple. What does this tell us about his attitude toward the Old Testament rites? How does 1 Corinthians 9:19–23 help us understand Paul's attitude?

3. What can we learn from 1 Corinthians 14:26–40 about the order or form of the earliest New Testament worship services? How would Paul respond to the idea that worship should not have a form or pattern?

4. What examples of externalism does Jesus give in Matthew 23? What is His attitude toward externalism? Why does He nevertheless say, "Therefore whatever they [the teachers of the law] tell you to observe, that observe and do" (Matt. 23:3)?

DISCUSSION GUIDE

1. What is the difference between form and formalism in worship? How do you respond to the idea that even "informal" worship has a form? Can you give some examples?

2. What are some of the continuities between the Old and New Testaments? What are some of the discontinuities?

3. What today draws some people toward as little structure in worship as possible? What draws other people to highly structured worship?

APPLICATION

1. Participate in a worship service and take note of the style, structure, and content of the service. Afterward, reflect on the ways you

believe these elements of the service aided and/or hindered genuine worship of the true God.

2. Thank God that He is the same yesterday, today, and forever—consistent from Old Testament times until now. How does it help you to know that His character is consistent?

CHAPTER 2

INTRODUCTION

The offering of sacrifice in the temple or tabernacle was the chief element of Old Testament worship. Christ offered Himself as the quintessential sacrifice for sin, so we don't offer animals on an altar in our worship. Yet sacrifice remains central to what worship is about historically, as far back as the time of Cain and Abel. The attitude of the one who offers a sacrifice is crucial. That attitude involves humility and trust in God alone.

LEARNING OBJECTIVES

1. To be able to explain the place of sacrifice in Old Testament worship, and especially in the worship of Cain and Abel.
2. To be able to explain why faith is essential to true worship and how this principle is illustrated in the story of Cain and Abel.

QUOTATIONS

For You do not desire sacrifice, or else I would give it;
You do not delight in burnt offering.
The sacrifices of God are a broken spirit,
A broken and a contrite heart—
These, O God, You will not despise.
—Psalm 51:16–17

So let each one give as he purposes in his heart, not grudgingly or of necessity; for God loves a cheerful giver.
—2 Corinthians 9:7

OUTLINE

I. *Latria*

    A. *Latria* is the Greek word most commonly translated as "worship" in the New Testament.

    B. In the Greek translation of the Old Testament *latria* is used for the practices of Israel's worship.

    C. The three basic components of *latria* in Israel were the offering of praise to God, the offering of prayer to God, and the offering of sacrifice to God. Worship was praise, prayer, and sacrifice.

    D. The most central element of Old Testament worship was going to the temple or tabernacle to offer sacrifices. Even praise and prayer were forms of sacrifice.

II. Christ and Sacrifice

    A. Christ offered Himself to God as the supreme sacrifice on our behalf.

    B. Therefore, in the New Testament era, we don't go to church and put animals on the altar as offerings to God.

    C. Yet offering sacrifice remains essential to what worship is about historically.

III. Sacrifice in the Time of Cain and Abel

    A. Vast sections of the books of Moses detail the sacrifices God commanded. Yet worship began much earlier.

    B. Adam and Eve worshipped in God's immediate presence before they sinned.

    C. Cain and Abel, the first generation raised outside Eden, offered sacrifice.

    D. Cain, the elder, was given the higher status of farming.

    E. Abel, the younger, was given the lower status of herding.

    F. Even though Cain had the more honored job, God "respected" Abel's offering but not Cain's.

    G. God nowhere said that a sacrifice from the flock was intrinsically superior to a sacrifice from the harvest.

    H. God accepted Abel's offering not because of its content but because of the offerer's attitude.

IV. Faith and Sacrifice

    A. Jesus affirmed this criterion (attitude vs. content) when He praised the widow who offered a tiny amount and not those who gave large sums (Mark 12:41–44).

    B. Paul said the Lord "loves a cheerful giver" (2 Cor. 9:7), and *cheerful* is an attitude of the soul.

C. Hebrews 11 tells us, "By faith Abel offered to God a more excellent sacrifice than Cain" (v. 4). Abel's faith made all the difference.

D. Abel's faith was in God's promise in Genesis 3:15 that the sacrifice of the Seed of the woman would destroy the Evil One.

E. The worship of God has always involved the spoken word of promise.

F. The word of promise was always accompanied by a tangible sign.

G. The word of promise in the Old Testament is the promise of the coming Redeemer who would offer a perfect sacrifice to save God's people from their sins. Redemption was tied to sacrifice.

H. Hearing the promise wasn't enough for Cain and Abel. The issue was whether they would trust the promise.

I. Cain trusted in his status as firstborn. God had no respect for trust in oneself.

J. Abel had nothing in this world on which to rely. He was only a shepherd. He trusted God's promise alone.

K. True *latria* begins in the soul.

V. Cain's Anger

A. God's judgment is always just.

B. Cain's anger at God's rejection of his offering was presumptuous.

C. Those who trust God's promises also trust His judgment.

D. Arrogant worship is a contradiction. God never owes us anything.

E. It is arrogant to assume that God is willing to receive any kind of worship people bring—Christian, Jewish, Buddhist, Hindu, etc.

F. A faithful person in Cain's shoes would have asked God's forgiveness for his or her sinful attitude and asked for a changed heart.

G. Those who are angry at God's judgment tend to hate the faithful as well.

VI. Conclusion

The single most important thing to understand about worship is that the only worship acceptable to God is worship proceeding from a heart that is trusting in God, and in God alone.

BIBLE STUDY

1. In Genesis 22, why does God ask Abraham to offer his son as a sacrifice? What role does faith play in Abraham's sacrifice? What additional insights does Hebrews 11:17–19 offer?

2. In Leviticus 1:1–9, what details about the burnt offering does God specify? What details are added in verses 10–13? In verses 14–17? This is just one of the many types of sacrifice specified in Leviticus.

What purpose(s) did all these details have? What do they tell us about Old Testament worship? About God?

3. *Atonement* is mentioned in Leviticus 1:4 as the reason for that type of sacrifice, the burnt offering. Atonement is also discussed in Leviticus 16, which describes the rites for the Day of Atonement (Yom Kippur). What is atonement? What is its link to sacrifice in these Old Testament texts? Make a list of significant details about the atonement sacrifice in Leviticus 16.

4. According to Hebrews 9:11–10:18, how has Christ fulfilled the promise of those Old Testament sacrifices? In what various ways does the writer compare Christ's sacrifice to those prescribed in Leviticus?

DISCUSSION GUIDE

1. How does the story of Cain and Abel illustrate the centrality of sacrifice in Old Testament worship? How does it illustrate the centrality of faith in that sacrifice?

2. Why is trust in God alone essential to true worship?

3. Why is it arrogant to assume that God should accept any kind of worship we choose to give?

APPLICATION

1. Sacrifice offered in faith was central to Old Testament worship. Jesus offered Himself as the ultimate sacrifice for sin. Give thanks and praise to God for that sacrifice. What response of trust can you offer?

2. If you have been angry, resentful, or ungrateful toward God, confess that attitude, and ask Him to create in you a clean heart and renew in you a right spirit.

CHAPTER 3

INTRODUCTION

Christ has offered Himself as the ultimate blood sacrifice for sin. We no longer offer dead animals to God. Instead, in light of all that Christ has done for us, our logical response, our reasonable *latria*, is to offer our own selves to God as living sacrifices. We offer everything we are and do to honor God.

LEARNING OBJECTIVES

1. To be able to explain what it means to worship in spirit and in truth.
2. To be able to explain what it means to offer oneself as a living sacrifice, and why we should do it.

QUOTATIONS

God is Spirit, and those who worship Him must worship in spirit and truth.
—John 4:24

I beseech you therefore, brethren, by the mercies of God, that you present your bodies a living sacrifice, holy, acceptable to God, which is your reasonable service [*latria*].
—Romans 12:1

OUTLINE

I. Sincere Praise

    A. We can tell the difference between genuine words of praise and insincere flattery. Flattery insults us.

    B. Insincere praise doesn't hurt God's feelings, but it doesn't honor Him either. True worship must be sincere.

    C. Genuine praise expresses honor, esteem, respect, and awe.

II. In Spirit and in Truth

    A. In saying the Father seeks those who will worship Him in spirit and in truth, Jesus meant that the location and substance of the sacrifice was less important than that is true (genuine) and spiritual (from the worshipper's spirit).

    B. Jesus Himself was always authentic in the honor He gave constantly to the Father.

III. Living Sacrifices

    A. Paul began Romans 12 with a passionate entreaty: "I beg of you …"

    B. His "therefore" means "in light of God's revelation of the righteousness made available to us by faith, in light of God's grace of election, I beg you for something that should flow out of that entire gospel."

C. He then said, "I beg you to present yourselves as a living sacrifice, a sacrifice that is holy, that is sacred, a sacrifice that is acceptable to God, which is your spiritual worship."

D. He meant, "What is your reasonable response to what Christ has done for you? It is to offer your life, yourself."

E. Offering ourselves means what we think, do, and how we live is all motivated by a desire to honor God.

F. Our motives are always marred by sin, but we can trust Christ our Mediator to present our offerings to the Father.

BIBLE STUDY

1. According to Jesus in Matthew 6:1–18, what is wrong with the way hypocrites give money, pray, and fast? Is doing these things in corporate worship a problem? Is it possible to do these things in the context of public worship without being a hypocrite? If so, how? If not, why not?

2. Numbers 6:1–21 explains how an Israelite could offer himself to God as a Nazirite, a special kind of devotion to God. What were the outward signs of this offering of oneself to God? What might have been the significance of these particular outward signs? How is the offering of oneself to God today similar? How is it different?

3. In Romans 6:12–19, Paul adds more to our understanding of what it means to offer our bodies as living sacrifices. What did he say

here that fills out our understanding of Romans 12:1? In what ways might we offer our *bodies* to God—and in fact the *parts of* our bodies to God? How might we offer our eyes? Our hands? Our mouths? What reasons for doing so does he give in this text?

4. In 1 Samuel 13:5–14, King Saul waits seven days for the priest Samuel to come to where the army is camped and offer a sacrifice before they fight a battle against the Philistines. After seven days, when Samuel doesn't show up, Saul offers the sacrifice. Why does he do that? How does Samuel respond when he arrives? Why? How would you describe Saul's attitude toward God? Toward the offerings made to God? How would you describe Samuel's attitude?

DISCUSSION GUIDE

1. What are some examples of ways a person might offer himself or herself to God as a living sacrifice?

2. If God doesn't like insincere worship, what should we do if we aren't feeling awe, honor, and esteem toward God? Should we avoid worship in that case? Explain.

3. Sometimes worship is used to "charge our batteries." If worship does not charge our batteries, should we still participate? Why or why not?

APPLICATION

1. Identify one way you can offer your mouth, hands, eyes, ears, feet, or yourself as a whole to God this week. Then ask for God's grace and take action.

2. Make a list of reasons why you should hold God in awe and esteem. Then write down anything that gets in the way of your awe and esteem for God. Pray honestly about what you've written, in thanksgiving, praise, petition, lament, and/or confession.

CHAPTER 4

INTRODUCTION

The temple in Jerusalem was meant to be a house of prayer. There was an altar in the holy place of the temple that was used exclusively for burning incense. The incense represented the prayers of the whole people rising up to God. Are our church sanctuaries houses of prayer? What form should the prayers of the gathered people have in our worship?

LEARNING OBJECTIVES

1. To be able to explain the role of corporate prayer in worship at the temple in Jerusalem.
2. To come to some conclusions about how our sanctuaries could be houses of prayer, and the forms that corporate prayer could have in our worship.

QUOTATIONS

Let my prayer be set before You as incense,
The lifting up of my hands as the evening sacrifice.
—Psalm 141:2

And the whole multitude of the people was praying outside at the hour of incense.
—Luke 1:10

My house shall be called a house of prayer.
—Matthew 21:13

OUTLINE

I. The Altar of Incense

    A. God ordained that there should be a second altar in the tabernacle and temple, in addition to the altar of burnt offering. This was the altar of incense (Exod. 30:1–9).

    B. The rising smoke of the incense symbolized the prayers of God's people ascending to His throne (Rev. 5:8; 8:3–4).

    C. In commanding the perpetual burning of incense, God was telling His people not to draw near to Him except in an attitude of prayer.

II. Prayer for and by the People

    A. The priest Zacharias had the privilege of presiding at the altar of incense to represent the people before God in prayer.

    B. He went to the altar of incense not to pray for himself but to deliver the prayers of the people. While he prayed for the people, they were gathered as a large body, and they also prayed.

    C. An angel told him God had heard his prayer for the people, and Zacharias's son would have a role in their redemption.

III. A House of Prayer
- A. Jesus made it clear that prayer was a central aspect of temple devotion when He said, "My house shall be called a house of prayer" (Matt. 21:13; Isa. 56:7).
- B. Jesus did not call the temple a house of sacrifices or a house of preaching. He called it a house of prayer. It was to be the focal point of the people for prayer.
- C. Do we think of our church buildings today as houses of prayer?

IV. Recovering the Emphasis on Prayer in Our Worship
- A. Prayer played a major role in the churches of the Reformation leaders.
- B. How can we as evangelicals recover that emphasis on prayer in worship?
- C. We can kneel when we pray. In the Old Testament, bowing and kneeling were the posture used in the presence of a king.
- D. We can involve the congregation in prayer led by the pastor, just as the people joined Zacharias in prayer. This involves directed prayer. The pastor directs the congregation to pray by name for various categories of people in need.

V. Conclusion

In ancient Israel, the primary function of worship was the offering of prayer. And so it should be in our churches today. Our sanctuaries should be houses of prayer.

BIBLE STUDY

1. Once a year on the Day of Atonement, the priest put some of the blood of the atonement sacrifice on the horns at each corner of the altar of incense (Exod. 30:10). Given the symbolism of the altar of incense, why would it need to have the blood of the atonement on it?

2. The psalms are the Bible's prayer book. They were used when the people gathered for prayer at the temple. Make a list of things the community prays about in Psalms 46; 65; 67; and 68. What are the community's priorities in prayer? How do they convey those things to God? What picture of corporate worship does Psalm 68 offer? How could the psalms be used to develop our vocabulary of corporate prayer?

3. What was the content of the prayer Solomon offered on behalf of the people when the temple was dedicated in 2 Chronicles 6:12–7:3? What did he ask for? What kinds of prayer did he foresee happening in the temple? What actions—by Solomon and by the people—accompanied that prayer? What was the point of kneeling?

4. What reasons for kneeling are given in Psalm 95:5–7; Mark 1:40; and Acts 9:40, 20:36; 21:5?

DISCUSSION GUIDE

1. How do you respond to the idea of the church building being a sanctuary for prayer? What sounds good, surprising, uncomfortable, challenging, motivating, etc. about that?
2. How do you respond to the idea of a whole congregation kneeling together to pray? What do you think that would convey to the people? How would it affect them?
3. What forms of corporate prayer have you experienced? By what criteria do you evaluate whether these forms are worthwhile to use?

APPLICATION

1. If you are in a position of authority or influence in your church, propose some ideas for corporate prayer based on your study of this chapter.
2. If you are not in a position to do that, pray for your church leaders to make wise decisions regarding corporate prayer.

CHAPTER 5

INTRODUCTION

God's communication to Israel was chiefly verbal, but He consistently reinforced His Word with nonverbal signs, symbols, gestures, drama, concrete object lessons, images, and rituals. Likewise, in the New Testament, Jesus reinforced His verbal communication of the gospel with signs and symbols. Why does God communicate through symbols, and how does He want to do so in our worship?

LEARNING OBJECTIVES

1. To be able to explain the difference between a sign and a symbol.
2. To be able to explain why symbols are important in our worship.

QUOTATION

Now it came to pass, as He sat at the table with them, that He took bread, blessed and broke it, and gave it to them. Then their eyes were opened and they knew Him; and He vanished from their sight.

And they said to one another, "Did not our heart burn within us while He talked with us on the road, and while He opened the Scriptures to us?" So they rose up that very hour and returned to Jerusalem, and found the eleven and those who were with them gathered together, saying, "The Lord is risen indeed, and

has appeared to Simon!" And they told about the things that had happened on the road, and how He was known to them in the breaking of bread.
—Luke 24:30–35

OUTLINE

I. Introduction: The Elements of the Lord's Supper Illustrate a Central Question
    A. We use bread and wine for the Lord's Supper because those are the elements Christ used.
    B. Historically, the church has tried to maintain a close connection with what Christ instituted.
    C. If we truly want to worship God in the way He directs, we should be willing to use those elements.
    D. Question: Why did God give such rituals to the church?

II. The Primacy of God's Verbal Communication
    A. God's communication to Israel was chiefly verbal.
    B. We therefore have a high view of the importance of God's verbal communication with us.
    C. We emphasize the role of the Bible as the Word of God.
    D. The pulpit, where the Word of God is preached, has historically been the focal point of Protestant sanctuaries.

III. The Link between Verbal and Nonverbal Communication
>A. Throughout redemptive history, God has always reinforced His verbal communication with nonverbal communication.
>B. He used a rainbow to enhance His verbal covenant with Noah.
>C. He used thunder, lightning, a cloud, and a trumpet sound to reinforce His covenant at Sinai.
>D. He commanded His prophets to use object lessons, such as Isaiah's nakedness.
>E. Israel's rites (sacrifice, incense, the priests' clothing, circumcision, Passover, etc.) were heavily symbolic.
>F. Humans naturally reinforce words with actions, such as shaking hands when we greet someone.
>G. John the Baptist reinforced his message with the sign of baptism.
>H. Jesus instituted Christian baptism and the Lord's Supper.

IV. Signs and Symbols
>A. The sacraments of baptism and the Lord's Supper are the signs and symbols of the New Testament.
>B. That is, they are exceedingly important nonverbal dimensions of full worship.
>C. A *sign* points beyond itself to another reality.
>D. A *symbol* is a sign that participates in the reality it points to. It is part of that reality.

E. The symbol escalates the sign's intensity to another level.

F. John Calvin emphasized that the elements of the Lord's Supper are symbols, not empty signs. The bread and wine are part of the reality we engage in at the Lord's Table.

G. Calvin said Christ is really—though not physically—present at Holy Communion. His divine nature and substance are really there.

V. Conclusion

Like the Reformers, we must never underestimate the verbal element of worship, but we must not forget that God also mandated tangible acts of drama that are married to the Word. The Word is expressed verbally, and then the drama of signs and symbols reinforces the verbal expression.

BIBLE STUDY

1. In Isaiah 20:1–6, why does God command Isaiah to walk around naked for three years? What does the word "sign" mean in verse 3? What is Isaiah's nonverbal action a sign of? How is the sign linked to verbal communication?

2. In John 13:1–17, why does Jesus wash His disciples' feet? What is this nonverbal action a sign of? How is it linked to verbal communication? How were the disciples expected to respond to it by word and/or action? How are we expected to respond? What evidence is

there in the text that this action is, or is not, a drama we should repeat on a regular basis?

3. In John 6:1–14, Jesus does something that John calls a "sign" (v. 14). What is the sign? What greater reality does it point to? How is the nonverbal sign linked to verbal communication in John 6:25–59? Would the verbal communication have had just as much impact without the sign? Why or why not?

4. You looked at Leviticus 16 in chapter 2. Now look at it again. Were the sacrifices on the Day of Atonement simply signs that pointed to a greater reality? Or were they symbols that participated in that reality? What is the evidence? See also Hebrews 8:1–6; 9:1–14; 10:1–10.

DISCUSSION GUIDE

1. What is the difference between a sign and a symbol? What examples can you give of a sign that is simply a sign, and one that is a symbol? Why does the difference matter in our worship?

2. What does it mean to say that the Lord's Supper is a symbol? How is it more than a naked sign? What is it a symbol of? How does it participate in that greater reality?

3. What has been your experience of nonverbal communication in worship? What, if any, forms of nonverbal communication have you valued? Why? How has this chapter affected your view of nonverbal communication in worship?

APPLICATION

1. Attend a worship service, and take note of all nonverbal communication you can observe in it. Notice what the architecture and interior design of the worship space convey about God and the gospel. Notice any visual art or the lack of it; what does it convey? How? What does the music, if any, convey? How does the music reinforce or work against the lyrics? Are there smells? What do the worship leaders do with their bodies? What do the members of the congregation do with their bodies? What does the clothing of the leader(s) convey?

2. Thank God for the signs and symbols by which He reinforces the Word of the gospel in your life. What specific signs and symbols are you especially grateful for, and why?

CHAPTER 6

INTRODUCTION

John the Baptist was the last and greatest prophet of the old covenant. He came as a prophet on the order of Elijah, renewing Elijah's office, to prepare the people for the Messiah. His baptism had its roots in Old Testament precursors. It is related to the baptism we undergo, but not identical to it.

LEARNING OBJECTIVES

1. To be able to explain the Old Testament precursors to our baptism.
2. To be able to explain the meaning of John the Baptist's baptism.

QUOTATIONS

Behold, I was brought forth in iniquity,
And in sin my mother conceived me.
—Psalm 51:5

[John said:] "I indeed baptize you with water unto repentance, but He who is coming after me is mightier than I, whose sandals I am not worthy to carry. He will baptize you with the Holy Spirit and fire."
—Matthew 3:11

OUTLINE

I. Introduction

    A. John the Baptist was the last and greatest prophet of the old covenant.

    B. The baptism we perform today is not identical with John's baptism. There is significant continuity, but also discontinuity.

II. The Seeds of Baptism in the Old Testament

    A. Baptism itself was not practiced in the Old Testament, but there were precursors.

    B. One precursor of baptism was the story of Noah. God used floodwaters to destroy the world but used that same water to save Noah and his family.

    C. Likewise, the Red Sea waters destroyed the Egyptians but saved the Israelites.

    D. Washing with water in the laver was significant in the Israelite liturgy. It symbolized the priests' need for cleansing from sin.

III. The Need for Cleansing

    A. Every baby is born into the world carrying the weight of the fallen human nature.

    B. Original sin was not the first sin; it is the *result* of that first sin. It is the fall of the human race into corruption.

IV. The Cleansing of Converts to Judaism
    A. We don't see a great emphasis on missionary outreach in the Old Testament, but the mandate is there.
    B. Non-Jews or "Gentiles" were considered unclean because they were outside the household of faith.
    C. For a Jewish male to be a true member of the household of faith, he needed to be circumcised as a baby and then undergo a profession of faith at age thirteen.
    D. For a non-Jewish male to become a member of the household of faith, he had to be circumcised, make a profession of faith, and undergo a cleansing ritual called proselyte baptism.
    E. In the book of Acts we read about God-fearers, Gentiles who had met all of the requirements of conversion except circumcision.

V. The Baptism of John the Baptist
    A. The last prophecy of the Old Testament promised that Elijah would return before the Messiah came.
    B. After four hundred years of prophetic silence, John came dressed and acting like Elijah, to be the forerunner of the Messiah.
    C. John told people to repent because the kingdom of God was about to come.
    D. John said the people needed to undergo the cleansing rite that was formerly just for Gentiles.

God was saying through John that His people were unclean.

E. John didn't want to baptize Jesus because he knew Jesus was the sinless Messiah.

F. Jesus insisted on being baptized because God had commanded baptism, and Jesus's life was about fulfilling all of God's commands as Adam had failed to do. Jesus was representing the nation.

G. Like John's baptism, our baptism signifies cleansing from sin and involvement in the kingdom of God. But our baptism has deeper meanings too.

BIBLE STUDY

1. According to Exodus 30:17-21, when did the priests need to wash in the laver? Why then? What would happen if they didn't? What do you think this penalty communicated?

2. Under what circumstances did nonpriests have to wash for ritual cleansing before approaching God in His tabernacle (Lev. 14:1–9; 15:1–33)? These circumstances weren't acts of sin, but were signs that represented ritual impurity. How would repeated ritual washing like this train the minds of those who went through it?

3. What role did washing in water play in the story of 2 Kings 5? What was its purpose? Leprosy was discussed in Leviticus 14:1–9. Why would leprosy be a vivid picture of sin? How is it relevant that the leper in 2 Kings 5 was a Gentile? What role did faith play in what happened in this story?

4. What do you observe about John and his baptism from the following texts: Luke 3:1–20; 7:18–35? What was John's message? What did "repentance" mean to him? What sort of actions did he expect would accompany repentance? Based on what evidence do we say that John was the greatest prophet of the old covenant?

DISCUSSION GUIDE

1. What is original sin? Why do we believe that babies are born with original sin? What difference does it make to our lives if we understand what original sin is?
2. How is the story of Noah a precursor of baptism? What does it mean to say that the Israelites were "baptized into Moses"? Why does it matter that there were Old Testament precursors to baptism?
3. How would you explain the meaning of John's baptism?

APPLICATION

1. Thank God that you have been cleansed from sin and made part of the household of faith. Tell God what difference that makes to you.
2. Is God calling you to any actions that are the fruit of repentance? If so, from what are you repenting, and what action do you need to take?

CHAPTER 7

INTRODUCTION

John's baptism was not a sign of a covenant. It was simply a sign of repentance given to Jews in preparation for the coming of the Messiah. Jesus instituted a baptism in the name of the Trinity as the sign of the new covenant, just as circumcision was the sign of the old covenant. What does it mean that baptism signifies the new covenant, and what else does it signify?

LEARNING OBJECTIVES

1. To be able to explain what baptism signifies.
2. To be able to define relevant terms like covenant, regeneration, and identification with Christ.

QUOTATIONS

Go therefore and make disciples of all the nations, baptizing them in the name of the Father and of the Son and of the Holy Spirit.
—Matthew 28:19

Unless one is born of water and the Spirit, he cannot enter the kingdom of God. That which is born of the flesh is flesh, and that which is born of the Spirit is spirit.
—John 3:5–6

OUTLINE

I. Baptism Is a Sign.

    A. It is *the* sign. In the old covenant, the sign was circumcision. In the new covenant, the sign is baptism.

    B. If we observe the outward sign and miss the significance, the sign is almost empty.

    C. So we need to understand and embrace the significance with our hearts.

    D. John's baptism was not a covenantal sign. It was simply a sign of repentance given to Jews in preparation for the coming of the Messiah.

    E. So what does New Testament baptism signify?

II. Baptism Is the Sign of the New Covenant.

    A. A covenant is an agreement that involves promises and obligations.

    B. In the Bible, a covenant is a promise of God, and the new covenant is God's promise of salvation through faith in the person and work of Jesus Christ.

    C. Baptism is the sign of every benefit God bestows on us in Christ.

    D. Circumcision had a positive signification and a negative signification.

    E. The positive signification was that God set apart the person receiving it and the Jewish nation. They were a people with whom God had entered into a redemptive relationship.

F. The negative signification was that the person said, in essence: "God, if I fail to keep the terms of the covenant, may I be cut off from all of Your benefits."

G. That dual aspect carries over into the new covenant. Positively, baptism is a sign of the blessings promised to those who receive Christ. Negatively, it is a sign of the curse that will fall upon us if we repudiate the terms of the new covenant.

III. Baptism Is a Sign of Rebirth.

A. We come into this world as fallen creatures, creatures of the "flesh" (*sarx*). Flesh is our corrupt human nature.

B. We are biologically alive, but we are in a sinful state that profits nothing, a state of spiritual death.

C. We need to be raised to new life in order to respond to God.

D. Unbelievers are never in a neutral state with respect to God. In their hearts, they are anti-God.

E. In regeneration (rebirth), God works on the soul of a person and changes the disposition of his or her heart. Regeneration is the antidote to original sin.

F. Baptism symbolizes that new birth. It is a sign of spiritual resurrection, of being brought from spiritual death to spiritual life.

IV. Baptism Is a Sign of Our Identification with Christ.
    A. Two aspects of Christ are signified by baptism: His humiliation and His exaltation.
    B. Christ was the first to be exalted by being raised from the dead, and all of those who are His will be raised from death, too.
    C. Christ is the "heir of all things" (Heb. 1:2), and we are "joint heirs with Christ" (Rom. 8:17). We will inherit a kingdom because we are in Christ.
    D. When God looks at us, He sees the merit of Christ.
    E. However, we share in His exaltation only if we are willing to share in His humiliation and suffering.
    F. To bear persecution or the natural afflictions of a fallen world as Christ did is to bear witness to His suffering.
    G. Our suffering does not atone for anyone's sin, but God's redemptive historical plan has to be finished, and that plan includes the afflictions of the people of God.
    H. Immersion is preferable to sprinkling, though not essential. The immersion process more graphically communicates our being buried with Christ in baptism and then raised.

V. Baptism Is a Sign of Salvation.
    A. It is a sign of cleansing from sin.

B. It is a sign of forgiveness, justification, sanctification, and glorification. It indicates everything involved in the process and the complete work of salvation.

   C. It is a sign of faith, repentance, and the baptism of the Holy Spirit.

VI. The Outward Sign Doesn't Guarantee the Inward Reality.

   A. This is true of baptism just as it was true of circumcision.

   B. We do it not because it guarantees regeneration but as a response to the promise of God. His promise of all these blessings, for all who believe, is signified by the sign our Lord instituted and commanded to be taken to all nations.

   C. When Satan comes to assault me, I can say, "I am baptized. I bear the sign of the promise of God." When I say that, I am saying: "I trust in this promise, Satan, for it is God's promise."

BIBLE STUDY

1. What do you observe in the following texts about the use and meaning of baptism in the book of Acts? Who was baptized? Why? What did it mean?

   Acts 2:36–47

   Acts 8:26–40

   Acts 9:1–19

Acts 10:44–48; 11:15–18
Acts 16:12–15, 29–34
Acts 19:1–7

2. How does Paul explain the meaning of baptism in Romans 6:1–14? How is baptism a fitting sign of what he describes? How does Paul expect his readers to live in light of their baptism?

3. How does Paul explain the meaning of baptism in Colossians 2:9–15? How does he want his readers to respond (2:16–3:17)?

4. How would you restate in your own words what Peter says about baptism in 1 Peter 3:20–22? (You might want to consult several translations and even a commentary, because this is a notoriously difficult Greek text to translate.)

DISCUSSION GUIDE

1. What is the new covenant? What does it mean to say that baptism is the sign of the new covenant? What is the positive signification of it? What is the negative signification? How are we meant to respond?

2. What is regeneration? What does it mean to say that baptism is a sign of regeneration?

3. What does it mean to say that baptism is a sign of identification with Christ? How do we identify with His exaltation? With His humiliation?

APPLICATION

1. Are you afflicted in any way? If so, how can this be an opportunity for you to identify with Christ in His suffering? How will that affect the way you deal with this situation? What will you say to God in prayer about this?

2. Thank God for all of the things your baptism signifies. Thank Him for regeneration. Thank Him for specific ways you will share in His exaltation.

CHAPTER 8

INTRODUCTION

Should the infants of believers be baptized? Or should the sacrament be restricted to those who are old enough to make a profession of faith before receiving baptism? There are arguments for and against each position, but they can't both be right. Either God wants believers to have their infants baptized, or He doesn't.

LEARNING OBJECTIVES

1. To be able to explain the arguments against infant baptism and for believers' baptism only.
2. To be able to explain the arguments in favor of infant baptism (in addition to baptism of adult converts).

QUOTATIONS

Then they spoke the word of the Lord to him and to all who were in his house. And he took them the same hour of the night and washed their stripes. And immediately he and all his family were baptized. Now when he had brought them into his house, he set food before them; and he rejoiced, having believed in God with all his household.
—Acts 16:32–34

For the unbelieving husband is sanctified by the wife, and the unbelieving wife is sanctified by the husband; otherwise your children would be unclean, but now they are holy.
—1 Corinthians 7:14

OUTLINE

I. Implication, Not Clear Command
    A. Nothing in the New Testament explicitly commands infant baptism.
    B. No New Testament narrative clearly indicates that an infant was baptized in the early church.
    C. But nothing in the New Testament explicitly forbids the baptism of infants or explicitly teaches that a profession of faith is a necessary prerequisite.
    D. There are passages that may teach these things by implication.
    E. Both sides on this issue can't be correct.

II. Arguments against Infant Baptism
    A. Since baptism is a sign of the faith of the person receiving the sacrament, only those who profess faith should receive it.
    B. The New Testament command to be baptized is articulated in these terms: "Repent and be baptized" or "Believe and be baptized." A very young child is not capable of exercising repentance

and faith because these are, at least in part, cognitive functions.

C. There are no examples of infant baptism in the New Testament. All twelve examples of baptisms in the New Testament involve adults and a prior profession of faith.

D. Historical records do not mention infant baptism until about AD 150.

E. The New Testament mode of redemption breaks down the Old Testament focus on ethnic continuity and biological inheritance.

F. When the church baptizes infants in whom no regeneration has occurred, people may be confused and conclude that baptism transmits regeneration.

G. Baptism as an adult experience is existentially more vital than that of an infant.

III. Arguments for Infant Baptism

A. An overwhelming majority of churches historically has favored infant baptism.

B. The Old Testament sign of faith, circumcision, was given to infants, so the New Testament sign of faith, baptism, should be given to infants as well.

C. Circumcision symbolized faith. Abraham received "believers' circumcision." But not only did he receive the sign of faith; he was commanded to circumcise his children. Isaac received "infant circumcision," the sign of faith.

D. If a sign of faith should not be given to someone who is not yet capable of demonstrating or exercising faith, then Old Testament circumcision must be condemned also.

E. The real question is whether the practice of including children of believers as recipients of the sign of the covenant carries on into, or was annulled by, the new covenant.

F. Churches that practice infant baptism also practice believers' baptism for adult converts. This also was true of circumcision for adult converts in the Old Testament. Yet infants in that era were given the sign of faith.

G. Infants may have been included in some of the baptisms recorded in the New Testament. The texts say, "So and so and his household were baptized." Some scholars say the Greek word translated "household" specifically does refer to children.

H. When the head of the family entered a covenant, his entire family received the benefit.

I. Paul says in 1 Corinthians 7:14 that our children have covenant privileges of being "set apart" and are not "unclean." If they are included in the covenant, why would they not be given the sign of the covenant?

J. After AD 150 infant baptism appears to have been the universal practice of the church, and we have no record of any controversy.

K. Salvation was never genetic. In the Old Testament no one was saved because he or she was a child of Abraham or Isaac. That was the heresy of the Pharisees.

L. The New Testament nowhere says that this aspect of the commanded covenant practice should be changed. God threatened to execute Moses when Moses delayed giving the covenant sign to his children.

BIBLE STUDY

1. What evidence does Romans 4:9–16 offer that circumcision was a sign of faith, and that Abraham received "believers' circumcision"? On the other hand, how would someone who thinks infants should not be baptized understand this passage?

2. Genesis 17:12–13 commands Abraham to circumcise not only infants biologically related to him, but also foreign slaves and their children who are part of his household but not of his ethnic group. What does that say about the meaning of circumcision in the old covenant? Is this relevant to the discussion of baptism? Why or why not? (See also Matt. 3:9; Rom. 2:28–29; Gal. 3:6–9. What do these passages indicate about whether the old covenant was based on ethnic inheritance rather than repentance and faith?)

3. What do you make of 1 Corinthians 7:14? In what sense(s) are the children of believers "sanctified" (set apart) as the children of unbelievers aren't? In what sense(s) are the children of unbelievers "unclean" while the children of believers are clean? What covenant

privileges do the children of believers have? What, if anything in your view, does baptism have to do with this?

4. Read Acts 16:15, 33 and 1 Corinthians 1:16 in their context. How would one go about researching whether "household" included small children or whether it referred only to those old enough to make a decision about whether they believed the gospel? Do some of that research and see what you find.

DISCUSSION GUIDE

1. Explain the argument that compares baptism to circumcision. How persuasive is to you? Why? In what ways are they alike, and in what ways are they different?

2. What is the argument that is based on the word translated "household"? How persuasive is this to you? Why?

3. How do you respond to the argument from history? Before AD 150 there are no surviving records of infant baptism and no records of any debate about it; after AD 150 there are widespread records of infant baptism and no records of any debate about it. What conclusions do you draw?

APPLICATION

1. Share with someone what you've learned about baptism from this book.

2. Pray for your children, and/or for the children of others. Ask God to include them in the household of faith and to bring them to maturity of faith.

CHAPTER 9

INTRODUCTION

There was probably nothing more important to the worship of the first generation of Christians than the celebration of the Lord's Supper. Christ Himself instituted this worship element. But Christians debate what the Lord's Supper means. They agree about its past and future meaning, but they debate its meaning for the present.

LEARNING OBJECTIVES

1. To be able to explain what Christians agree is true about the past and future meanings of the Lord's Supper.
2. To be able to explain the four views of what the Lord's Supper means for the present.

QUOTATIONS

And He took bread, gave thanks and broke it, and gave it to them, saying, "This is My body which is given for you; do this in remembrance of Me."

Likewise He also took the cup after supper, saying, "This cup is the new covenant in My blood, which is shed for you."
—Luke 22:19–20

The cup of blessing which we bless, is it not the communion of the blood of Christ? The bread which we break, is it not the communion

of the body of Christ? For we, though many, are one bread and one body; for we all partake of that one bread.
—1 Corinthians 10:16–17

OUTLINE

I. The Past Dimension of the Lord's Supper: We remember what Jesus did on the cross.

II. The Future Dimension of the Lord's Supper
    A. Jesus said, "I will no longer eat of [the Passover meal] until it is fulfilled in the kingdom of God" (Luke 22:16).
    B. The Lord's Supper points forward to the marriage banquet of the Lamb, when we will feast with the King (Rev. 19:7–9a).
    C. It is a foretaste of that ultimate fellowship we will have with Him in heaven.

III. The Present Dimension: Four Views of How Christ Is Present
    A. What did Jesus mean when He said, "This *is* My body" and "This *is* My blood"? Is there a real identity between the bread and the wine and Jesus's body and blood, or is there simply a symbolic representation?
    B. The Roman Catholic Church teaches that during the prayer of consecration, a miracle takes place in which the ordinary elements of bread and wine are

supernaturally changed into the actual body and blood of Christ, though they continue to appear outwardly to be bread and wine. Therefore, the person who is communing is actually participating in the body of Christ physically.

C. Martin Luther denied the miracle, but he insisted on the substantial presence of Christ at the Lord's Supper. Luther was concerned that people would reduce the elements to empty or naked signs. The bread stays bread, and the wine stays wine, but underneath them, hidden from our view, is a real union of the body and blood of Christ with the elements. Christ is truly there substantially touching His human nature as well as His divine nature, so that we truly feed upon the body and blood of Christ in His glorified humanity at the Lord's Table.

D. Ulrich Zwingli's view is probably the most widely held view among evangelical Christians today. It holds that there is no real substantive presence of Christ in the Lord's Supper; rather, the whole event is a sacramental drama wherein the elements remain merely important signs and symbols. Zwingli said there is a representation of Christ in the bread and the wine, but there is no substantial presence of Christ's body and blood at the Lord's Table.

E. The Reformed view was articulated by John Calvin. Calvin denied the physical presence of the body and blood of Jesus in the Lord's Supper. However, Calvin argued for the real presence of Christ in the sacrament. Christ is really there at the table. We fellowship with Him in His real presence. But Calvin also said that the presence of Christ is in no way tied to the elements themselves. And he said that the physical presence of Christ is not immediately localized at the Lord's Table.

IV. The Council of Chalcedon and Calvin's View

    A. At the Council of Chalcedon (AD 451), the church fathers declared that Christ is truly man and truly God.

    B. Christ's two natures are united without mixture, confusion, separation, or division, each nature retaining its own attributes. When God in His divine nature unites with the human nature, the divine nature does not give away its divine attributes, and the human nature does not stop being human. When Jesus was hungry, His human nature was hungry. We can distinguish between the human and the divine in this way, but even when Jesus was hungry with respect to His humanity, His human nature was still perfectly united with the divine nature.

    C. In His divine nature Christ can be at more than one place at the same time, but in His human nature He can't. Although Jesus's human nature is always and everywhere perfectly united with His divine nature, only the divine nature can be everywhere at once. The Heidelberg Catechism states, "Christ is true man and true God. With respect to His human nature He is no longer on earth, but with respect to His divinity, majesty, grace, and Spirit He is never absent from us."

D. Calvin said the body and blood are in heaven because they are part of Jesus's human nature, which is localized. But the human nature up there is perfectly united with the divine nature, which is not limited to any one locale. When we celebrate the Lord's Supper here on earth, we are communing with Christ in His divine nature. In this act of mystical communion with the divine presence of Christ, the human nature of Christ is made present to us.

E. Jesus at the Lord's Supper is saying, "You are coming to My house for dinner, and I am going to give you that kind of concentration of intimacy and assurance that goes with it." Jesus sits down with His people to give them special attention and to dispense a particular grace to them. He comes to comfort them, forgive them, and strengthen them.

BIBLE STUDY

1. In what ways is the Lord's Supper connected with the feast discussed in these texts?
    Isaiah 23:6–8
    Matthew 22:1–14
    Revelation 19:7–9a

2. What can we learn from 1 Corinthians 11:17–34 about what the Lord's Supper means? How was it done in Corinth at that time? What problems were the Corinthians having with it, and how did Paul want them to correct those problems? What does it mean to be "guilty of the body and blood of the Lord" (v. 27)?

3. In Matthew's account of the feeding of the five thousand, Matthew said Jesus took the loaves and fish, blessed them, broke the loaves, and gave them to the disciples (Matt. 14:19). In his account of the Last Supper, Matthew said Jesus took bread, blessed it, broke it, and gave it to His disciples (Matt. 26:26). Is the repetition of the four verbs (took, blessed, broke, gave) coincidence, or are the two accounts linked in some way? If they are linked, how? If not, how can you tell? (Consider comparing the accounts of these events in the other gospels. In some translations the verb "blessed" is rendered as "gave thanks.")

4. Read all of Matthew 26. Note places where Jesus' divine nature is active and places where His human nature is active, yet He remains one person.

DISCUSSION GUIDE

1. What is the future meaning of the Lord's Supper? How is it important to us now?

2. Which of the four views of the Lord's Supper are you most familiar with? Which of them do you find persuasive? Why? How do you believe the Lord's Supper benefits us?

3. What does it mean to say that Christ is truly man and truly God? How is this relevant to our understanding of the Lord's Supper? How is it relevant to our understanding of what Christ did on the cross?

APPLICATION

1. Participate in a celebration of the Lord's Supper. As you do so, reflect on what Christ did for you in the past, on what you are looking forward to in the feast in the kingdom of God, and on Christ's presence with you at the table.

2. Ask Christ to help you know Him more fully as truly man and truly God.

CHAPTER 10

INTRODUCTION

The number one reason people give for leaving church is that it's boring and irrelevant. But nobody who has experienced the presence of God has ever described it as boring and irrelevant. So the reason people find church boring is that they have no sense of the presence of God there. And if they have no sense of His presence, how can they be moved to worship Him?

LEARNING OBJECTIVES

1. To be able to explain the importance of a true sense of God's presence in worship.
2. To be able to explain the importance of engaging both the mind and the body/senses in worship.

QUOTATIONS

O God, You are my God;
Early will I seek You;
My soul thirsts for You;
My flesh longs for You
In a dry and thirsty land
Where there is no water.
So I have looked for You in the sanctuary,

To see Your power and Your glory.
—Psalm 63:1–2

And when I saw Him, I fell at His feet as dead.
—Revelation 1:17

OUTLINE

I. Why Some People Find Church Boring
   A. In the Bible, when people encounter God, they weep, cry out in terror, tremble, fall on their faces. They are never bored or say, "That was irrelevant."
   B. A Christian worship service is an encounter with God.
   C. But when people attend and have no sense of God's presence, they find it boring.
   D. The crisis of worship today is that people need a true sense of God's presence.

II. What Is Permissible in Worship
   A. People throughout history have lacked a sense of His presence, and they have often resorted to idolatry, which is an attempt to make God visible in ways that are unacceptable to Him.
   B. John Calvin was concerned about God's prohibition against images in worship. He rejected the Catholic *douleia* (service) of icons, images, and statuary because he saw it as worship.

C. The question of images is part of the broader debate over what is proper worship. Some churches say that anything that is not prohibited in Scripture is acceptable. Others say that only that which is authorized by Scripture is legitimate.

D. We are looking at the Old Testament for principles to guide us because it gets us out of speculation and preferences. Only in the Old Testament does God Himself explicitly demand that certain things take place in worship.

III. Engaging the Mind in Worship

A. Jesus's emphasis on truth (John 4:23–24) in worship means that the mind must be actively engaged. Worship is not simply an experience of feeling.

B. That is why Protestant worship gives so much attention to the reading and preaching of the Word of God.

C. But we risk becoming Gnostics who think our response to God is purely mental.

D. The mind is not enough.

IV. Engaging the Whole Person

A. None of our experiences are purely intellectual. Human life involves the mental and the physical.

B. The body is the threshold of the mind for everything that exists outside of us.

C. Then the mind must process the information collected by the senses.

D. Therefore, we are not to approach worship as if we were disembodied minds.

E. Neither are we to come to worship with skepticism, saying, "I cannot see, hear, smell, touch, or taste God; and unless I can experience God with my senses, it does not matter what logic says to me, I will not believe that He exists."

F. In the Old Testament the whole person—mind and senses—was involved in worship.

G. The Old Testament puts limits on how we can use our senses in worship. It prohibits graven images.

H. Yet Israel's worship was intensely visual.

I. It was also strongly auditory with music and hearing the Word read.

J. There was also incense to smell.

K. In the New Testament, in addition to the Word we have singing and the sacraments, which appeal to nearly all of our senses.

L. The rest of this book will look at how the Old Testament engaged the senses in worship and how we might do so.

BIBLE STUDY

1. How do the people in the texts below respond when they encounter God? Why do they respond that way? Should we expect to have experiences like this? Why or why not?

> Genesis 17:1–3
> Exodus 3:1–6
> Exodus 20:18–19
> Isaiah 6:1–7
> Luke 5:1–9
> Revelation 1:9–17

2. When the psalmist in Psalm 63:1–5 speaks of seeing God in the sanctuary, what do you think he means? Have you ever had the kind of thirst for God that he describes in verse 1? Have you had the satisfaction of the soul that he describes in verse 5?

3. What body postures for worship are described in these passages? What reasons for these physical expressions are given? In what ways, if any, are these relevant today? On what basis can we decide if they are relevant and how?

> Nehemiah 8:6
> Psalm 28:2
> Psalm 134:2
> Psalm 47:1
> Psalm 95:6–7
> Psalm 149:3

4. The Jews of Jesus' day had their identity tightly wrapped up in the temple in Jerusalem, and there is a thread in the New Testament that reacts against that. What attitudes toward the temple do the following texts express? How have these affected the way modern Protestants view church buildings?

> Luke 21:5–6
> Acts 7:48–49
> John 2:18–22
> 1 Corinthians 3:16
> Ephesians 2:19–22

DISCUSSION GUIDE

1. How regularly do you experience the presence of God in worship? How would you describe that experience, or lack of it? What do you think we are supposed to experience?

2. Are you tempted to overemphasize the life of the mind? Of the emotions? Of the senses? If so, how? What do you do about that?

3. In what ways do the worship services you typically attend involve your mind? In what ways do they involve your sight, your hearing, your sense of smell, your body posture?

APPLICATION

1. Attend a worship service that is different from the ones you usually attend, in a building different from the kind of building you usually worship in. Notice the physical space and how it affects the worship experience. Notice what you see in artwork (or the lack of it),

architectural features, banners, furnishings, what the worship leaders wear, and so on. Notice the body postures people use. Notice what you hear, and how the music, words, and other sounds affect the worship. Does the worship engage smell or taste or touch?

2. Ask God to help you experience His presence in worship. On the other hand, sometimes God deliberately withdraws the sense of His presence for a time so that we can experience walking by faith without feeling, and in those times we can actually experience the otherness of God through His absence. Therefore, it might be equally valuable to ask God to help you know Him in His absence. But if you've never experienced His presence, ask for that.

CHAPTER 11

INTRODUCTION

With good reasons, Christians are ambivalent about beauty in worship. We're troubled about spending money on a sanctuary rather than on missions or the poor. We're concerned that images and even buildings can become idols. We want churches to be inviting places for fellowship. Yet there are good reasons for making our worship reflect the "beauty of holiness," the glory of God Himself.

LEARNING OBJECTIVES

1. To be able to explain how visual beauty was involved in Old Testament worship, and why.
2. To be able to discuss how worship today could reflect the good, the true, and the beautiful without leading people to idolatry.

QUOTATIONS

One thing I have desired of the LORD,
That will I seek:
That I may dwell in the house of the LORD
All the days of my life,
To behold the beauty of the LORD,
And to inquire in His temple.
—Psalm 27:4

HOW THEN SHALL WE WORSHIP?

Give to the LORD the glory due His name;
Bring an offering, and come before Him.
Oh, worship the LORD in the beauty of holiness!
Tremble before Him, all the earth.
—1 Chronicles 16:29–30

OUTLINE

I. Beauty as Nonverbal Communication

    A. Beautiful things can function as tokens that express love, value, and esteem.

    B. We are creatures who respond to what we see.

    C. Seeing people bowing before statues communicates something particular to us.

    D. Seeing an empty room with no pews, statues, tables, books, or carpeting also gives a visual experience.

    E. Every building has some kind of form, so whenever we go to a worship service, we have a visual experience that communicates something particular.

II. Beauty in the Tabernacle

    A. There may be nothing in Scripture to which God devoted more minute detail of description than the tabernacle.

B. Jewels and other valuable goods were used to create a worship space that was not only functional but beautiful (Exod. 25).

C. God gave infinite care to the design of worship space (Exod. 26).

D. God gave detailed instructions about the priests' garments because He wanted them to communicate God's glory and beauty (Exod. 28:2b).

E. God may still care that worship of Him communicates His glory and beauty, "the beauty of holiness" (2 Chron. 20:21; Pss. 29:2; 96:9).

III. The Good, the True, and the Beautiful

A. God is the source and standard of everything good. We are called to reflect who He is by doing what is good.

B. All truth is holy because all truth ultimately comes from God. He is the essence of truth.

C. Just as God is the standard for the good and the true, so He is the ultimate standard of beauty.

D. Revelation 21 describes the splendor of the New Jerusalem. In heaven the church will be beautiful, as well as good and true.

E. God wants the worship offered to Him to be good—that is, holy—and not evil. True worship must be done righteously.

F. God is not honored by false teaching and lies. There must be a commitment to truth at the heart of our worship.

G. Likewise, even though we are far removed from the old-covenant rites, it appears to be consistent with the biblical pattern that we who live under the new covenant also should be concerned that our worship bear witness to the glory of God and to the beauty of holiness. It seems appropriate for our worship to be conducted in beautiful spaces with beautiful accouterments.

IV. Beauty versus Other Priorities

A. A Gothic cathedral may cause us awe but also ambivalence about the trappings.

B. St. Pierre's in Geneva is plain in terms of ornamentation, but its architecture proclaims the transcendence of God.

C. Protestants have sought to rid church buildings of things that might entice people to idolatry. They adopted plain robes for their ministers. They avoid anything that smacks of Roman Catholic tradition.

D. Church design today emphasizes the congregation's comfort to encourage fellowship. Buildings designed for fellowship follow a form that does not communicate the glory and beauty of God.

E. Some church buildings are designed to look like town meeting halls, not overtly houses of worship.

F. We have gone from chancel, pulpit, and congregation to stage, lectern, and audience.

G. The idea is to show that worship comes from the heart, not from external stimuli.

H. Some feel we should spend money on missions or the poor, not on a sanctuary.

I. Others say, "We want the sanctuary to be beautiful. We want it to be a place that expresses our desire to honor the magnificence of God."

J. When building a church, we are always tempted to re-create the Tower of Babel, a monument to ourselves. We need to remember that a church should communicate God's glory.

K. Whatever we do should be done with a view toward making the church building a visible expression of our desire to honor God—in the architecture and in the adornment. Even what the pastor wears will have an impact on the people's worship experience.

L. I sometimes wonder whether we are more concerned about decorating our own bodies and our own homes than we are about honoring God in worship.

BIBLE STUDY

1. Read these texts closely, and pause to mentally picture what the various components of the tabernacle looked like. Picture the colors, the metals, the gems. What would it be like to worship in a tent with these colors and metals?

    Exodus 25:1–7
    Exodus 26:36–37

2. Read Revelation 19:9–21 closely, and pause to mentally picture the walls made of gems. If you don't know what some of the gemstones are, you can find pictures online. What is this meant to convey about the Holy City? About God?

3. How does Matthew 26:6–13 convey the tension between spending costly sums on worship versus spending it on the poor? What reason for spending lavishly on worship does it express? Is this text intended to say that we should always choose to spend on worship rather than on the poor? Why or why not? How does Isaiah 58 express the other side of this tension?

DISCUSSION GUIDE

1. Why do the form and appearance of worship spaces matter? What do the form and appearance of your worship space communicate? How does your church deal with the tension between competing priorities: worship, fellowship, mission, care for the needy?

2. Why does the clothing of worship leaders matter? What does the clothing of your worship leaders communicate? God's glory and beauty? Something else?

3. Why are Christians often ambivalent about beauty? What does "the beauty of holiness" mean? How important is that to you? Why?

APPLICATION

1. Ask the Lord how He wants your church to reflect the beauty of holiness, His own glory and beauty. Ask Him to protect you from idolatry and self-glorification, but rather to display His beautiful splendor.

2. Talk with others in your church about visual beauty in your worship space. Share with them what you've learned from this chapter, and invite them to think with you about how to balance beauty with fellowship, missions, and compassion.

CHAPTER 12

INTRODUCTION

Music is a powerful form of communication. Christians debate the musical styles that are good for worship, the use of instruments, the content of lyrics, and even whether there should be music at all. What can we learn from the Scriptures about these things?

LEARNING OBJECTIVES

1. To be able to explain how music was used in worship in the Old and New Testaments.
2. To be able to discuss principles for making decisions about "good" music and "good" lyrics for worship.

QUOTATIONS

Praise Him with the sound of the trumpet;
Praise Him with the lute and harp!
Praise Him with the timbrel and dance;
Praise Him with stringed instruments and flutes!
Praise Him with loud cymbals;
Praise Him with clashing cymbals!
Let everything that has breath praise the Lord.
—Psalm 150:3–6

STUDY GUIDE

Let the word of Christ dwell in you richly in all wisdom, teaching and admonishing one another in psalms and hymns and spiritual songs, singing with grace in your hearts to the Lord.
—Colossians 3:16

OUTLINE

I. Musical Instruments in Worship

    A. Psalm 150 says it's possible—even commanded at that time—to worship God with trumpets, cymbals, and other instruments.

    B. Since nothing in Scripture contradicts Psalm 150, we infer that it is at least permissible to use musical instruments in worship.

    C. Some Christian groups believe using musical instruments in worship is inherently evil, but in Psalm 150 God approves their use.

    D. Some Christians believe only organ or piano is permitted, but historically the organ's purpose was to imitate the sound of an orchestra in churches that couldn't afford an orchestra.

II. Singing in Worship

    A. Israel sang in worship from its earliest time (Exod. 15) through to the time of Nehemiah (Neh. 12). The psalms were written to be sung. Singing was a vital part of Old Testament worship.

B. In the New Testament, Jesus and His disciples sang a hymn on the night He was betrayed (Matt. 26:30).

C. In heaven, the Lord is going to give His people a new song (Rev. 5:9).

D. Luke records songs related to Christ's nativity.

E. The range of the human voice is one of the things that differentiate humans from animals.

F. We can say God is like a mighty fortress, or we can sing "A Mighty Fortress Is Our God." The altered mode of conveying the words affects us emotionally.

G. We must use our God-created ability to sing for His glory.

III. Defining "Good" Music

A. It's arrogant to think that all the good church music has already been written.

B. It's also a mistake to think that the only good music is new music.

C. Many classic hymns were once innovative, sometimes shocking.

D. Worship music styles have often come from popular musical forms.

E. Thomas Aquinas and Jonathan Edwards said that criteria like harmony, proportionality, and complexity can be used to judge the quality of all types of artistic compositions, including music.

F. Music written today will go through the sifting process of time. Some will vanish, but others with the majestic measure of beauty will endure.

IV. Lyrics

A. Much of the theology people learn in church comes not from classes but by osmosis from what they sing over and over. Therefore, lyrics can be helpful or harmful.

B. The theology in most—but not all—traditional hymns is outstanding.

C. At least one Reformed denomination sings only psalms for Sunday worship, because the psalms were inspired by God, so there is no danger of bad theology in their words.

D. We not need to go that far, but whatever we sing must be consistent with the Word of God. The beauty of worship is never to be divorced from the truth of worship.

E. The best church music conveys a sense of God's transcendence. Music in worship should not familiarize God to us; rather, it should stimulate the soul to a posture of adoration.

BIBLE STUDY

1. What theology about God is conveyed in the lyrics of the songs in Exodus 15:1–21? How is the theology reinforced by the poetry of the

lyrics—by the figures of speech (such as calling God a warrior and imagining Him with a right hand, nostrils, and so on) and by the structure (such as reinforcing an idea with parallel lines: "glorious in holiness / fearful in praises")? Why does a song like this often have an impact on worshippers that preaching alone may not have?

2. What impression of God would the instruments described in Psalm 150:3–5 have conveyed? Why would God have wanted that? How would those instruments have been suitable to convey the theology of Psalm 150:1–2? How might the music for singing Psalm 131 be similar and/or different?

3. Study some of the song lyrics of heaven in the texts below:

>Revelation 5:9–10
>Revelation 5:12–14
>Revelation 15:3–4

How are these lyrics like the psalms? How are they different? Why will singing be appropriate for heaven? Why aren't the citizens of heaven simply singing the psalms?

4. Nehemiah 7:66–67 tells us that when the exiles returned to Jerusalem and rebuilt the temple, the city's total congregation was 42,360 people. For this size of group, they had 245 singers for worship. The community was far from rich. This was the one worship center for the city, and there were worship services every day. What can we learn from these figures, if anything, that is relevant to us?

DISCUSSION GUIDE

1. How was music used in Old Testament worship? In the New Testament?
2. What do you think about criteria for "good" worship music, such as harmony, proportionality, complexity, consistency with biblical truth, and a sense of God's transcendence?
3. What should we do in response to the strong and differing views people have about music in worship? What would be a constructive response in your context? What are the alternatives to fighting?

APPLICATION

1. Thank God for music. Thank Him for giving humans the ability to compose, play, and sing. Thank Him for musicians and music that have meant something to you, and tell Him what you value about that music. Whether or not you're a good singer, take time to worship God through music.
2. Search online for worship music you're unfamiliar with. For example, if you're unfamiliar with old worship music, search for Palestrina, Tallis, William Byrd, Bach, or Handel. What sense of God do these composers convey? Why do you think people are still singing their music centuries later? Or go to a site that has hymns, or one that offers the latest praise bands. What does this music convey about God?

CHAPTER 13

INTRODUCTION

Touch, taste, and smell communicate powerfully. Old Testament worship was full of the smell of incense, the taste of lamb and bitter herbs, the feel of animals and grain offered in sacrifice. We need to recover touch, taste, and smell in our worship.

LEARNING OBJECTIVES

1. To be able to explain the roles of touch, taste, and smell in Old and New Testament worship.
2. To explore the roles of touch, taste, and smell in worship today.

QUOTATIONS

Oh, taste and see that the LORD is good.
—Psalm 34:8a

And behold, a leper came and worshiped Him, saying, "Lord, if You are willing, You can make me clean."
    Then Jesus put out His hand and touched him, saying, "I am willing; be cleansed." Immediately his leprosy was cleansed.
—Matthew 8:2–3

STUDY GUIDE

OUTLINE

I. Touch in Worship
    A. Human beings need to be touched.
    B. Because the pastor represents Christ to his congregants, when he shakes hands with them after the service, it represents the touch of Christ.
    C. The New Testament practice of the laying on of hands is rooted in the Old Testament anointing with oil.
    D. The outpouring of oil on kings, priests, and prophets indicated a transfer of divine grace for the office.
    E. To indicate that transfer of grace, New Testament leaders laid hands on those whom they ordained for ministry. Many churches still do this.
    F. In the Old Testament, God gave a specific blessing He wanted the priest to say over the people. In the New Testament, the pastor touched people when he said the blessing or "benediction."
    G. Today when churches are larger, the pastor usually says the benediction to the whole congregation with upraised hands but without touching each person.
    H. In some churches, people who want prayer are able to go forward and receive a blessing with a touch on the head.
    I. Jesus often touched people when He healed them.

J. There is an art to shaking hands after the service. Elderly people, especially widows, need extra touch, so the pastor should take their hand in both of his.

II. Taste in Worship

A. The biblical writers often use taste as a metaphor to convey truth.

B. God designed the Old Testament feasts to use taste—bitter herbs, unleavened bread, lamb—to communicate truths.

C. In the Lord's Supper Jesus used bread and wine to communicate about His redemptive act. When we celebrate this sacrament, we taste the bread of life.

D. Wine suggests the bitterness of Christ's suffering and the joy of His marriage feast.

E. Many churches use grape juice instead of wine for the Lord's Supper to protect people from temptation to alcoholism, but the taste of grape juice doesn't convey all that the taste of wine does.

III. Smell in Worship

A. Memories of fragrances linger and provoke strong associations.

B. In the tabernacle, the altar of incense—made with a distinctive formula used only for worship—symbolized prayer.

C. The biblical writers use sweet and foul scents as metaphors for goodness or hypocrisy.

IV. Conclusion

To honor God as God, we must worship Him as He decrees. We must work to remove the shadows we have placed over the glory of God, so that God's people may be renewed by basking in His splendor.

BIBLE STUDY

1. What did the priests experience through touch when they were ordained, according to Exodus 29:4–9? How might these tactile memories have affected them and stayed with them?
2. How is the laying on of hands used in these texts?

> Numbers 8:10–12
>
> Mark 5:23
>
> Acts 8:14–17
>
> 1 Timothy 4:14; 2 Timothy 1:6

3. How is anointing used in James 5:13–14?
4. What instructions for the food of Passover does God give in Exodus 12:1–19? What tastes did those foods involve? Why did it matter that every year, down the generations, the same food with the same tastes would be eaten?
5. Exodus 30:34–38 specifies the exact formula for the incense used in worship to represent prayer. Why do you think God was so

specific about the formula? Why did He forbid the people to use that formula for any other purpose?

DISCUSSION GUIDE

1. How was touch used in worship in the Bible? How was taste used? How was smell used?
2. What role do you believe the laying on of hands should have in worship today? Why? What about anointing, or another tactile element from the Bible? What about other aspects of touch, such as shaking hands or hugging?
3. What are the pros and cons of making the Lord's Supper a more prominent element of worship today?

APPLICATION

1. Observe a worship service, and notice the use of taste, touch, and smell—or the lack of it. What do you observe? How does it affect the worship experience? How could taste, touch, or smell increase the sense of God's splendor?
2. Thank God for your sense of touch, taste, and smell. Ask Him how your church's worship can manifest the splendor of God more fully. Pray for those who plan and lead the worship at your church, and for the congregants who are also active worshippers, not audience.

WHY DOES IT MATTER WHAT JESUS DID?

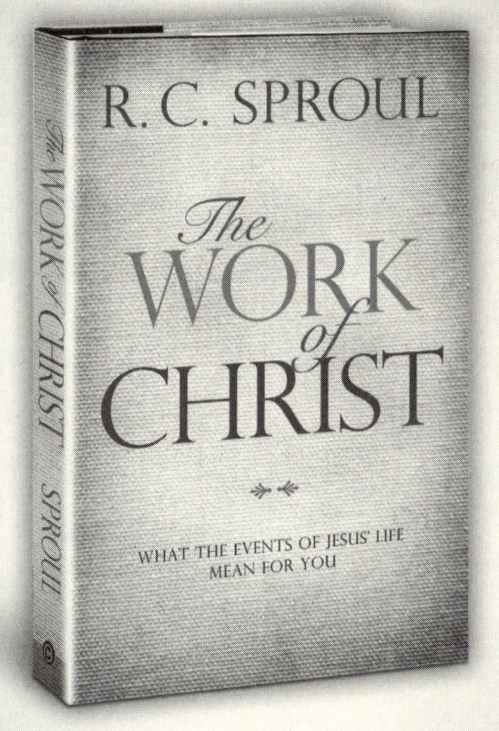

R. C. SPROUL

The WORK *of* CHRIST

WHAT THE EVENTS OF JESUS' LIFE MEAN FOR YOU

Dr. R. C. Sproul looks at the purpose behind Jesus' actions, addressing such life-changing topics as why Jesus' baptism is relevant for our salvation, why Jesus' ascension makes a difference in our lives today, and what we know and don't know about Christ's return. As you delve into the life of Christ, you will find renewed wonder at the Savior who loved you before time began.

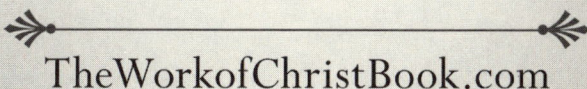

TheWorkofChristBook.com

David C Cook
transforming lives together

ALSO AVAILABLE IN EBOOK EDITIONS

Are you taking two steps forward and one step back?

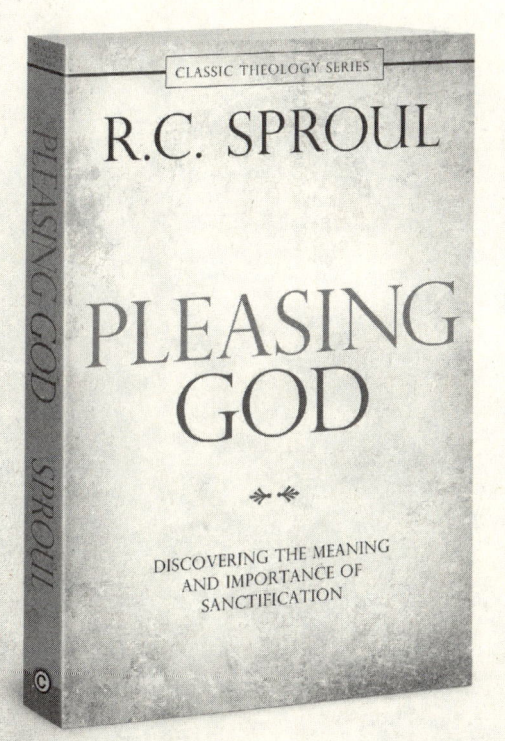

CLASSIC THEOLOGY SERIES

R.C. SPROUL

PLEASING GOD

DISCOVERING THE MEANING AND IMPORTANCE OF SANCTIFICATION

Our struggle to overcome sin in our lives can sometimes feel futile. Yet we can experience freedom from the challenges we face. In this landmark book, renowned teacher Dr. R. C. Sproul shares how we can experience genuine growth and change.

David C Cook
transforming lives together

ALSO AVAILABLE IN EBOOK EDITIONS.

Encounter a God who not only loves but is love.

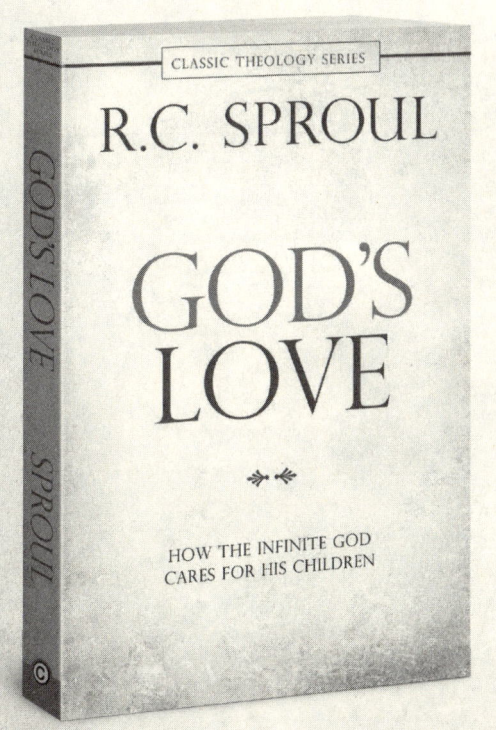

The greatest expression of love is found in our Savior. In *God's Love*, formerly released as *Loved by God: Can the Creator of the Universe Really Care about Me?*, Dr. R. C. Sproul takes an in-depth look at the nature, character, and unrelenting love of God.

David C Cook
transforming lives together